T0129258

EXECUTION

The Discipline of Doing Simple Things Consistently and Well

by

John Walton

authorHOUSE®

AuthorHouse™
1663 Liberty Drive
Bloomington, IN 47403
www.authorhouse.com
Phone: 1 (800) 839-8640

© 2016 John Walton. All rights reserved.

No part of this book may be reproduced, stored in a retrieval system, or transmitted by any means without the written permission of the author.

Published by AuthorHouse 03/29/2016

ISBN: 978-1-5049-8725-7 (sc)
ISBN: 978-1-5049-8726-4 (hc)
ISBN: 978-1-5049-8724-0 (e)

Library of Congress Control Number: 2016904878

Print information available on the last page.

Any people depicted in stock imagery provided by Thinkstock are models, and such images are being used for illustrative purposes only.
Certain stock imagery © Thinkstock.

This book is printed on acid-free paper.

Because of the dynamic nature of the Internet, any web addresses or links contained in this book may have changed since publication and may no longer be valid. The views expressed in this work are solely those of the author and do not necessarily reflect the views of the publisher, and the publisher hereby disclaims any responsibility for them.

Preface

Throughout our life we witnessed people take on personal challenges or engage in activities that require special effort beyond the daily run-of-the-mill tasks. Some of these endeavors are self-imposed while others are the result of situations we find ourselves in.

Many of these challenges are very visible to the public, while others can be of a very private or personal nature. Regardless of their nature or origin, the need to be engaged and accomplish or overcome these challenges is a fundamental part of life.

In almost every situation, these challenges, obstacles, trials, or strategic endeavors have that common thread that they require the very best of our abilities. Usually, these are not things that come easy or can be easily dismissed as unimportant. In almost every case, there are consequences if the effort is not made, or proper attention applied to the task. Some measure of success is almost always imperative.

While some of these endeavors may involve a considerable commitment of time and effort, most are things that take only a moment or two, or maybe a few minutes of our attention. Typically the maximum duration involved in any one task is less than a few hours a day. However it is the efficiency and effectiveness of our execution during those brief intervals of time that ultimately determine the success of the final outcome.

We know that it is our individual ability to execute that determines how successful we will be, however it has been my observation that what people typically struggle with is identifying and improving a small set of specific behaviors that when applied in any endeavor significantly impact their ability to achieve a successful outcome.

The word *execute* has frequently been used in describing the personal effort applied to how we accept and take on challenges. What is interesting is how the act of executing is described regardless of whether the outcome of the activity succeeds or fails. Consider how at the end of a sporting event when the team captains, coach's, or outstanding players of the game are interviewed, each will describe the outcome of the event in terms of the ability or inability of individual players or the team collectively to execute. So, what does that mean?

Both teams talk about their need to execute, but ultimately one team will come out victorious over the other. The winner's ability to execute was simply more successful at increasing their score verses their opponent. The question becomes; how did they accomplish that?

Studies show that upon a closer examination it seems that several behaviors and practices always exist that result in a more effective or efficient outcome that subsequently influences the outcome toward achieving success.

The question we need to be asking then is; what do efficient and effective people do when executing that ineffective and inefficient people apparently do not?

This book answers that question by exploring simple behaviors people perform and perform well who are more efficient and effective in their pursuit of success.

This book will also introduce ways to develop those behaviors, in order to make your execution in every situation consistently better.

About the Author

John Walton began his professional career as a software development engineer with a Bachelor's of Science degree from the University of Utah in Computer Science. Following graduation he climbed both the technical and management ladder at several of the world's top technology companies.

In 2001 John earned Project Manager Professional certification, and with the exception of a brief period operating his own consulting company has been working in program and project management roles for various consulting and contract organizations.

During his career John contributed to and helped direct the development of multiple technologies that have had a positive influence in the quality of people's lives throughout the world in areas of healthcare, defense, aerospace, financial services, banking, energy, communication, and semi-conductor design.

Over the last fifteen years he has shared his expertise by helping several small start-ups as well as large multi-national organizations eliminate wasteful practices and become more efficient in their day to day operations.

John's interest in achieving more efficient and effective execution began while working in program and project management. It was while reviewing project performance and reflecting on past experiences that he first began identifying fundamental behaviors that separated individuals who execute with an average level of effectiveness from those people who were truly exceptional performers.

This specific contribution to the topic of execution is based on his independent research coupled with thirty-five years of personal observations and first-hand experience managing people and activities.

Outside of his career, John has coached young women's softball in the local community's league, and has worked extensively in the Boy Scouts of America organization over a period of several decades serving at the local unit level as a Scoutmaster and in the district as an Assistant District Commissioner.

Mr. Walton currently lives in Northern Utah with his wife. They have six children.

Acknowledgements

My wife Candace and my children have been a great strength to me during the period over which this material was gathered and written. My love and thanks go to them for their patience and understanding.

In addition I would be remiss to not acknowledge the contributions of all the people who throughout history have inspired and encourage us to be the best we can in all that we do. Such a list is obviously too long to include.

Contents

PROLOGUE

The Battlefield

When evaluating the outcome of daily activities, we consistently discover that it is our ability to effectively execute those tasks over which we have control that determines our success.

The date was the 20th of February 1815. The sun was bright and helped take the oceanic chill out of the air of the early afternoon. The smell of salt water filled the air and invigorated the senses of the ship's hard working men and officers. Originating from across the distant horizon a steady stiff breeze lifted across the deck a fine spray from waves that broke against the solid wooden hull of the renowned American warship *USS Constitution* nicknamed Old Ironsides.

---

[1] The Painting by Charles Robert Patterson depicts USS Constitution exchanging broadsides with the HMS Java. 29 Dec. 1812

The United States was at war with Great Britain and Ireland over a variety of issues brought about by the British war with France which had caused trade restrictions between France and the United States and impressment of 10,000 American Merchant sailors into the British Royal Navy, among other things.

Having previously broken through the British blockade at Boston Harbor, *Constitution* was now sailing in Atlantic waters near the island of Madeira off the coast of Spain near the Mediterranean Sea. Throughout the quiet morning the crew had spent their time adjusting lines, and making never ending repairs to the heavy canvas sails that strained against the constant force of nature's wind.

The ship and its crews mission was to seek out British convoys in order to both replenish the ships own stores, and also capture or destroy British war supplies. Unfortunately, with long distance communication being what it was at this period in history, the ship's captain and crew were completely unaware that a peace treaty between the United Kingdom and the United States had been ratified three days earlier.[2]

At 1:10 PM, from atop the tall masts a lookout spots sails two points off the larboard bow. Closer examination reveals this to be a British warship. In light of their mission, and to relive the boredom that often accompanies the general daily activities aboard a war ship, a decision was made to give chase. Captain Charles Stewart orders the *Constitution* be fitted with full sail, and within moments the able bodied crew begins climbing the rigging. They quickly extend every foot of the ship's available heavy canvas so as to catch the powerful wind, and close the distance between the two ships.

Constitution alters course to engage the newcomer, and within a few minutes the identity of the still distant British ship becomes

---

[2] The Treaty of Ghent, signed on December 24, 1814 in the city of Ghent officially ended the War of 1812 between the U.S. and United Kingdom. The UK parliament signed the treaty into law on December 30, 1814. A month passed for the treaty to reach the United States where it was ratified by the U.S. Senate on Feb. 18, 1815.

certain. It is the thirty-four gun British frigate *HMS Cyane*. Word quickly spreads among the crew. Soon the mood of the entire ships personnel has changed to apprehension and excitement as the prospect of combat grows. During the next few hours the distance between the ships diminishes, and each order begins to take on greater urgency.

Knowing he has an advantage in both size and firepower, Captain Stewart gives orders to pursue the *Cyane* in earnest. With every inch of fabric deployed the bow of the ship crashes through the waves as if driven by a storm, producing great droplets that fall upon the decks like a torrential rain, yet the skies overhead are largely clear.

To maximize her speed, *Constitution's* sails are regularly trimmed to increase their efficiency causing the tall masts to creak under the growing pressure exerted on the crowded canvas sails that are stretched to full capacity. For some time, the groaning sounds of strained masts seemed to speak with the voice of howling demons. Suddenly, under this growing stress *Constitution's* main royal yard begins to crack. To avoid complete breakage, the ship is forced to slow as the crew makes repairs while still endeavoring to maintain pursuit.

During the next hour, while still managing to close the gap between the two war vessels, a second set of white sails and rigging of another ship are spotted against the horizon. The new comer is *HMS Levant*, a 20 gun British frigate that has been sailing these waters with the *Cyane*. Their captain's orders are to protect two merchant convoys that sailed from Gibraltar only a few days earlier.

Being smaller, the two British ships are more maneuverable, but they lack the necessary canvas to increase their speed and run from the formidable American vessel. Knowing this fact, they will have no choice but to fight.

While *Constitution* bears down upon them, the two British ships draw to within hailing distance of each other, enabling Captain Gordon Falcon on the *Cyane* and Captain Douglass on the *Levant* to converse.

The two captain's strategy is to delay their confrontation until after nightfall, then engage the larger American vessel which they have discovered to be the superior *USS Constitution,* but as time passes it will be clear that *Constitution* will close the gap before nightfall. Their jointly conceived plan was to combine their strength and attack in a manner with the objective of disabling the larger American ship, by leveraging their maneuverability and combined firepower.

By 2:30 P.M. the situation becomes very clear to Captain Stewart. The *Constitution* will be facing the pair of British warships whose captains intend to test the well-known American vessel in battle.

Of course at this distance the two challengers would not know that *Constitution's* main royal yard was damaged and that her running was not an option, but even if she could run the *Constitution* was built for battle. Reputation and honor demanded that the American warship accept the challenge to fight.

On all three ships, preparations for battle had begun. Orders were being shouted out by the officers to ensure powder and other armaments get distributed to the crew. Cannon were being readied and primed for the anticipated action. All non-essential equipment had to be stowed or secured and decks cleared of any item that might become a distraction or interfere with the crew's ability to fight.

Together the two British ships bring a combined fifty-five guns to bear against *Constitution's* fifty-four.[3] The problem Captain Stewart faces is how to best the two enemy assailants in a manner that will eliminate their combined gun advantage in a way where he can leverage *Constitution's* superior ability in one-on-one confrontation.

---

[3] *Cyane* was armed with 22 32-pounder carronades, 10 18-pounder carronades and two 12-pounder long guns, the slightly lighter *Levant* had 18 32-pounder carronades, 2 6-pounder long guns and a shifting 12-pounder. *Constitution* carried a main battery of 30 24-pounder long guns, and 20 or 22 32-pounder carronades and two long bow-chasers

Over the next four hours, *Constitution* will close the remaining distance while still making repairs to stabilize the damaged main royal yard. As the ships come into cannon range, the two English vessels draw together and form lines for battle, each seeking an opportunity to bring all possible fire power to bear on the American vessel.

Finally, at 6:10 P.M. with the winter sun's glow just dropping below the horizon, at a distance of approximating 250 yards, the first round of firing commences. Broadsides from all three ships are unloaded. Constriction's advantage in the number of long guns proves decisive against the lighter structure of the two British vessels.

Onboard the *Constitution* is Mr. A. Y. Humphreys who is serving as the ships chaplain. As the ship comes under fire, he begins to record a minute by minute account of the battle, recording the ship's officers shouting of battle orders in competition with the increasing roar of cannon fire. As one not specifically trained in the art of naval warfare he is non-the-less impressed with the ability of *Constitution's* well trained crew to execute each command with precision, and wonders whether it will be a determining factor in the ultimate outcome of the battle.

Humphreys describes in his account how Captain Stewart neutralizes the enemy's numerical advantage by maneuvering the larger war ship so as to be under fire from only a single enemy vessel at any given moment, thereby maximizing his advantage in fire power, and subjecting the British warships to repeated raking broadsides.

Still, despite Captain Stewarts careful maneuvering, the two English ships respond extremely well, moving quickly and repeatedly to reposition themselves in order to obtain a more advantageous position. By doing so the British ships well-directed cannon fire strikes the American vessel's hull more than she has ever been hit before.

A lesser ship may have succumbed to the constant pounding unleashed by the two British vessels, but *Constitution* was built to take such punishment. Most of the British cannon balls simply bounce off her sides solidifying her nickname, "Old Ironsides".

The battle rages on as the sun disappears over the horizon. The darkness of night slowly deepens revealing a vast constellation of stars in the heavens, their brilliance occasionally marred by the drifting smoke of rifle and cannon fire. As the moist ocean air cools, an increasingly dense mist settles on the waves, with ghostly wisps separated only by an occasional brilliant flash of light from cannon fire.

Amid the increasing darkness the days previously strong winds calm. Visibility diminishes with the increasing abundance of smoke mixed fog coupled with the smell of burnt powder. Unable to see his enemy clearly, Captain Stewart finds it necessary to cease firing in order to allow the smoke to disperse and there-by re-acquire the two enemy ships that constantly shift their locations in the hope of somehow disabling the American vessels ability to maneuver.

All three captains know the fog makes it possible to withdraw and quietly slip away, but being warships withdrawal is not in their nature. Still, just thirty minutes into the battle, the badly damaged Levant draws away to take stock of its situation and affect a few critical repairs. Ten minutes later at 6:50 PM, with the *Cyane* badly damaged and on its own against *Constitution*, Captain Gordon Falcon reluctantly strikes *HMS Cyane's* colors thereby surrendering his ship and crew to Captain Stewart. It was a painful act for Captain Falcon, and performed only in the interest of preserving the sea worthy integrity of the ship as well as the lives of its devoted crew.

Knowing the second British ship is close by Captain Stewart orders some of his officers and crew to quickly secure the HMS Cyane so he can refocus his attention back on the *Levant* which at that moment is courageously returning to the battle completely unaware that Captain Falcon has surrendered the *Cyane*.

At 8:00 PM, and hidden within the now dense surface mist and lingering smoke, the crews of the *HMS Levant* and *Constitution* sit quietly at their battle post, each man listening for any sight or sound of the opposing ship. It might be the flap of a sale, moaning of a mast, or the splash of a rogue wave against the hull of a moving ship. What each man fears is that it will be the sound of an enemy officer shouting the order to fire ships cannons.

Finally at 8:50 PM that order is given, and in this final exchange *Constitution* unloads two full broadsides before *HMS Levant* turns aside to run. *Constitution* gives chase and at half-past ten, out gunned and facing overwhelming superior fire power, Captain Douglass and his crew surrender the *HMS Levant* to Captain Stewart and *Constitutions* crew.

While Captain Stewart begins transferring captives, the crews of all three vessels take stock of the battle's outcome.

A spectacle of grim destruction appears in the now pale moonlight washing over the battered ships. The decks of the two English vessels that hours earlier were polished and secured are now littered with debris created by the sweeping fire of *Constitution's* powerful guns. They resemble slaughterhouses, shrouded in shattered wood railings, spilt powder, burned and torn sail, tangled rope, discarded weapons, and the grizzly bloody mangled bodies of dead and wounded sailors. It will take days to clear the wreckage from the deck, inventory materials, and make repairs.

Multiple histories record that during the battle *Constitution* suffered four dead and eleven wounded, and that two of the wounded would eventually succumb to their wounds.[4]

By comparison, losses from the two British vessels whose unconfirmed combined crews ranged in number from 260 to 320

---

[4] The Naval War of 1812, Theodore Roosevelt, New York Modern Library

officers, ship's crew, marines, and boys, included 40 dead, and nearly eighty wounded.[5],[6],[7]

Securing this extremely large numbers of prisoners and providing reasonable accommodation for officers while operating all three vessels was problematic for the American ships officers. In the days that followed both British captains and members of their crew would escape or simply be set free as *Constitution* sought to avoid further encounters by leaving the area.

Sometime later a court martial would be held according to British military tribunal for the purpose of investigating the actions of Captains Falcon and Douglas with respect to them surrendering their ships during this engagement. After careful consideration of the various armaments and recognition of the respective firepower of all three war ships, both men were honorably acquitted. They and their crews were recognized for the courage they exhibited, and the stout defense each of the British ship's crew made against a superior opponent.[8]

Interestingly enough, a few histories describing this engagement also record that rather than give the American's credit for their well-executed gunnery and Captain Stewarts tactical maneuvering, the two British captains, gallantly attribute the loss of their ships to their own mistakes. In essence, the American's did not defeat these men and their crews, but rather they defeated themselves.

Why is this fact noteworthy?

Despite the recognition that one-on-one their ships were over matched in every way for a one-on-one encounter, the two British

---

5 Enclosure in Captain Stephen Decatur to Secretary of the Navy Benjamin Crowninshield, dated May 1814, National Archives, Record Group 45, Captain's Letters Sent, 1815, Vol. 3, No. 93.

6 Indiana University, Lily Library, A.Y. Humphrey's journal, Humphreys Manuscripts.

7 Naval History and Heritage Command, Capture of Cyane and Levant, 1815 Old Ironsides' Battle Record: Documents of USS Constitution's Illustrious Deeds

8 Navel Occurrences of the War of 1812, William James, 2004

officers still believed that together they had the means to achieve victory. Both men attributed the loss of their ships during this battle to a failure on their part and the part of their crews to efficiently and effectively *execute* both as a crew and individually, thereby allowing the Americans to control the battle and inflict damage that otherwise might have been avoided.

Therein lays a great truth. Plans, strategy and tactics, no matter how well thought out, rely on the ability of individuals to execute in a manner that is both efficient and effective.

****

INTRODUCTION

The Art of Execution

Every great breakthrough came about because someone looked beyond traditional thinking.

What is it that separates an exceptional performance from an average performance? What distinguishes a master from his apprentice? What characterizes a craftsman, from an amateur? What defines an artisan from the common laborer? What sets a leader apart from followers? How is one person a powerful communicator while others stumble to express an idea? Why does a great plan fail, while a poorly conceived plan mysteriously succeed? Why do some people consistently achieve well deserved accolades of praise and recognition for their endeavors, while others lack even an honorable mention?

Ultimately, the answer to these questions comes down to whether persons set themselves apart by demonstrating the ability to execute efficiently and effectively. Execution is an art, and like every talent it can be enhanced. The question is how does one improve the ability to execute? What behaviors influence an individual's efficiency and effectiveness?

There is global acceptance in virtually every field of competition that the final outcome of any endeavor will be achieved by that team or individual who is able to execute to the highest level of proficiency.

Regardless of the objective, executing well is basic for achievement in all of life's challenges. Those who develop the fundamentals skills to execute well typically excel far beyond being average. They become champions, and heroes in their field. Mastery at execution is the secret of legends.

Over the past half century the topic of execution in business circles has risen to higher and higher levels of awareness. Corporate boards of companies such as Apple, IBM, Hewlett Packard, General Motors, Bank of America, and Yahoo, when replacing a CEO will stress to the new leader the need to improve the company's ability to execute.

In the field of sports as players and coaches discuss the outcome of a game the dialogue revolves around individual player's ability to execute to their maximum level of proficiency, but like the weak link in a chain, one weak performance can have disastrous consequences for the team.

The best strategies, tactics, plans, and processes are of little value if not well executed. Over and over again, the message is increasingly clear.

> *Success in any endeavor is dependent on the ability to execute to the highest level of proficiency.*

ORIGIN OF THE WORD EXECUTION

The word, *execute* originates from medieval times. It is derived from the Latin word E*xsequi* which is a compound word formed by the prefix "ex" meaning after or to follow, and "sequi" meaning sequence. Compounded, the word means a sequence that follows. Similar expressions of the meaning are; to complete, fulfill, or carry-out to the end.

The English expression of the word, "Execute" was popularized in the early British judicial system with respect to the administering of judicial matters. Execution of a court order accommodated a wide set of judicial actions ranging from a defendant being released or paying a fine, to public humiliations, imprisonment, or even death, for which numerous means existed, some of which included gruesome methods of torture.

In this latter case, the word actually served to avoid warning a prisoner of their impending date with death, or possibly arousing public outcry by a prisoner's friends. It also helped reduce any general outcry to the more torturous practices associated with graphic words like; whipped, shot, hung, or decapitated. The court would simply request that their written order be *executed.*

The medieval *executioner* was a court servant designated to carry-out the court's sentence *to its completion*. With the court order in hand, the unsuspecting prisoner could easily be escorted away from the court room not knowing their ultimate fate until they were either released, arrived at the prison, or brought to the town square where chains, stocks, gallows, or other public punishments were performed. The order was then *executed* according to the appointed method.

Like many merchant trades where skills were taught through an apprenticeship, the position of court executioner was often passed down from father to son. This rite of passage might include handing down a special axe, knife, whip, thumb screw, or other devices designed to inflict pain, or employ a punishment.

The profession included comprehensive training on practices related to carrying out the various forms of punishment according to approved policies and procedures. The executioner was not at liberty to simply execute the court order according to some personal convenience. There would be written directives that were approved, documents created dated and properly recorded, notices in some cases posted for the public, various arrangements completed as necessary for housing or feeding the convicted individual, and in some cases construction of facilities appropriate for the prescribed punishment, such as stocks, cages, or a prison.

Torture practices were obviously not designed to protect the rights of the accused people, but were used by corrupt and power seeking government officials to justify the seizing of individual's personal property or to instill fear in the populace so as to quiet public opposition. In some cases, the court order required practices intended to force a confession from the accused individual as justification for punishment.

When innocent people were executed in error or for political advantage, the accused individual's friends or family often sought revenge on the executioner for fulfilling the courts sentence. As a means of protection from reprisal, the executioner's identity was often concealed under a cloak and hood. Fear of retribution was so great that many an executioner had to be threatened into carrying out a sentence.

Of course sometimes a sentence was *not executed* as specified. Public officials could be bribed or opponents would erect barriers that prevented the ordered sentence from being executed, resulting in a *failure to execute*. Over time the phrase, *failed to execute,* has become a part of our language, just as *execution* has taken on a broader meaning.

Today, the concept of execution has evolved beyond simply carrying out judicial orders, and become common language relative to how every type of effort is carried-out.

* * * * * *

EXECUTION AS AN ABILITY

Despite the growing recognition of the importance of executing well, it is interesting that there is no standard for measuring this ability or to develop it as a specific talent. Rather execution is treated as a potpourri of best practices.

So where are the principles and skills for effective execution taught and practiced? Let's look at a few possibilities.

Parenting has always been the fundamental place for instruction, and as many a parent can attest, there is no manual on how to raise a child. Every parent develops their own approach. Outcomes are as varied as the approaches.

How about as part of a professional trade?

Consider family names such as Archer, Baker, Butcher, Cook, Carpenter, Fisher, Smith, Shoemaker, etc. Like the court Executioner these names once identified the respective trade of an artisan or craftsman whose skills were taught and passed down from father to sons or mother to daughter. The problem here is that skills in one trade do not necessarily transfer to other trades. Execution must therefore involve something more than proficiency in a specific skill or trade.

In our modern world technology is constantly evolving and in some cases has entirely replaced the human worker. Many once common professions and skills are being lost or forgotten. How many individuals know how to use a slide rule instead of a calculator? Who remembers calling the switchboard operator, or riding an elevator controlled by a person? Still, while technology can greatly improve productivity, dependency on technology can often have a diminishing impact on our ability to execute when we rely too much on it to accomplish an objective.

How about religion? Is execution taught in churches?

No! Religions focus on teaching values and practices that provide a moral compass, not the behaviors specific to the acts of executing.

What about academic institutions?

From elementary level through high school our methods of measuring student performance consist largely of comparing student test scores against some academic standard. Unfortunately, many an intellectual genius is ineffective when called upon to execute outside the academic framework. Execution requires an ability to analyze and apply knowledge, not simply recall information.

Most colleges and universities focus on transferring the knowledge associated with various arts or sciences such as physics, chemistry, etc. While lab work is included in many courses of study, it doesn't teach the underlying behaviors used when executing a task. Developing the behaviors to execute is left up to the school of hard knocks.

So if not in academia, how about in the business world?

I quick informal survey will show that few corporations invest in any form of internal training for their employees, let alone in the specific discipline of execution. Instead, today's businesses strive to hire individuals who already possess effective execution abilities. It is not surprising to find that most businesses are finding it difficult to find qualified people. Why? Just because a person is familiar with a business concept or technology, doesn't mean they are effective when it comes to executing.

When all is said and done, most people will conclude that the fundamental abilities associated with executing are simply acquired through practical experience and developed in real world scenarios.

While somewhat true, it is unfortunate that these behaviors are exercised and developed in a relatively inconsistent manner. The results are outcomes that are equally inconsistent.

The reality is that developing the ability to execute to one's maximum potential is in almost all cases left completely up to the individual to discover, develop, and apply on their own.

In those few cases, where an ability to execute effectively is taught, the simple behaviors involved are not obvious and outcomes are unpredictable.

* * * * * *

DISCUSSION ON EXECUTION

The topic of Execution has been discussed by ancient philosophers, business executives, respected consultants, world-class athletes, coaches, researchers, and writers for centuries. The list of contributors is filled with the names of successful individuals and high profile professionals with international name recognition. Their contributions to this subject and the on-going dialogue are greatly valued.

With no intention of downplaying these contributions, it is important to note that most of the existing material does not actually focus on the act of *execution* per-'se. Most contributions examine various strategies, processes, tactics, tools, or methods in an attempt to *manage* events to achieving a desired outcome.

A lot of books and publications focus on tactics and strategies to be effective at only a few specific activities, but by learning to execute well your results are going to be more effective in every area.

Many contributors recommend activities like;

1) Writing down goals and reviewing them regularly.
2) Using reflection and meditation to be inspired.
3) Creating lists, and checking off accomplishments.
4) Developing a personal mission statement.
5) Using a personal planner and prioritizing activities.
6) Leveraging modern technology.
7) Networking to develop stronger relationships.

These suggest tasks to do, but not how to do those tasks better. While these are excellent practices that contribute to success they don't apply to the act of execution per-'se.

Remember, ***what*** we do is not the same as ***how*** we do it. Execution is about being both efficient and effective at **how** we do things.

In a management study conducted in 2007, the CEO's and executive leaders of various organizations were asked to define execution. The study itself is of no particular note except to point out that participant's responses all fell into some common categories with answers like;

- Execution is a phase for doing the planned work.
- Execution is about exceptional performance.
- Execution focuses on goals and achieving results.

These are not bad answers, but when then asked, "How is execution actually done?" these CEO's faces grew blank.

Curious about this type of response, I conducted a similar study from professionals in the International Project Management community.

Project Managers are at the front lines working directly with people who *do* the actual work to deliver a product or service. For them, execution is a key factor of success. The question asked was simply, "How do you define execution?"

The overwhelming tendency of responders was to identify a process phase targeting ***what*** tasks need to be done. This was not particularly surprising, since this thinking is espoused to the general project management community in the Project Management Body of Knowledge.[9] Certified project managers are taught to view execution as a specific phase involving various activities that should be performed.

Others responders suggested execution involved applying industry best practices which on the surface are attempts to suggest *how* to make execution more effective, but ultimately redirect attention to *what* constitutes a best practice.

In the end, nowhere did this group actually suggest *how* to execute in ways that maximize effectiveness.

Several years ago Dr. Lawrence G Hrebiniak, a management professor with Wharton School at the University of Pennsylvania,

---

[9] A guide to the Project Management Body of Knowledge (PMBOK Guide) Fifth Edition, published by the Project Management Institute

published an article discussing why good business strategies fail.[10] The article states that "MBA-trained managers know a lot about how to formulate a plan, but very little about how to carry it out", and that despite being good managers, "they really have to learn through the school of hard knocks, through experience".

The problem with experience is that accumulating pertinent real world knowledge and turning it into a skill requires considerable time and unfortunately often is obtained more through failure than success. Someone once said;

> *"Those who attend the school of hard knocks rarely graduate soon enough to apply their wealth of experience toward achieving anything meaningful".*

Waiting a lifetime to execute effectively is not acceptable in today's fast paced society. People need to fast-track their acquisition and ability to execute at maximum effectiveness.

With that brief introduction let's examine what execution is, and is not, and hopefully dispel some of the erroneous concepts people cling to.

DEFINING EXECUTION

First of all, execution is not a strategy or tactic. It is not some new process, scientific methodology or paradigm. It is not a mind expanding theory embraced by a small group of zealots. It is also not a collection of mysterious secrets once hidden away and only recently discovered in some lost parchment written in a forgotten language used by ancient people.

Execution doesn't require the use of performance boosting drugs. It is not a product created using essence extracted from an exotic fruit

---

[10] Making Strategy Work Leading Effective Execution and Change, Wharton School Publishing

grown in remote rainforests. It can't be brewed, or baked, swallowed, absorbed, inhaled or injected. It isn't a pill, gel, cream, charm, potion, or magic spell that enhances individual performance.

Execution cannot be outsourced or off-shored, mitigated or delegated, expensed or deducted, purchased or sold. The work activity itself might involve these things, but how the endeavor is actually executed does not.

Execution is nothing tangible. It is however observable and its efficiency and effectiveness measureable.

Now that we've clarified what execution is not, let's look at what it is. Let's begin with a very simplistic definition.

Execution - To Do

Execution is defined not in terms of whom, what, where or why, but rather in terms of how. In this sense, how do we achieve the targeted objective? *We do it.*

Short and simplistic, the definition sets forth a very important concept;

Whatever you ***do*** must actually get done. If whatever ***it*** is doesn't get done, then the act of execution failed.

The free online dictionary by Farlex supports this concept.

Execution - The carrying out of some act or course of conduct to its completion.

The problem with these two definitions is they don't offer any insight to explain how to consistently execute so as to achieve objectives. Simply completing a task doesn't indicate whether any particular standard of quality was achieved. Many times things get done, but they get done poorly.

A proper definition must therefore consider how well the effort satisfies the objective. Consider this story.

In 1947 Howard Hughes, the owner of Hughes Aircraft and Trans World Airways corporation, took on the task of building a unique airship for the United States military.

At that time the United States was fighting World War II. Tasked with carrying critical war supplies to Europe, America's commercial merchant ships were easy targets for the packs of German U-boats patrolling the Atlantic Ocean.

The primary objective of the project was to build a merchant ship that could fly. It would land and take-off in water and be capable of carrying heavy armored vehicles or other war materials across the Atlantic.

The proposed vessel was named Hercules, and upon completion was characterized as the world's largest flying boat.

Designed by Henry Kaiser, the Hercules is huge. It stands five stories high, has a wingspan longer than today's Boeing 747 and is powered by eight engines.

With the war raging, aluminum, the preferred material for the ships construction, was in demand for military aircraft. As a commercial ship, alternative materials had to be found. Plywood was the material chosen.

When stakeholders first saw the Hercules prototype, many wondered if the air ship could even take off, let alone carry heavy loads of cargo. The challenges grew daily and cost overruns forced Hughes to invest millions of dollars from his personal fortune into the endeavor.

To demonstrate the plane would hold together, the prototype was flown by Mr. Hughes himself a distance of several miles along the coast of California. Despite this successful demonstration, it was to be the aircrafts first and only flight.

The demonstration failed to inspire stakeholders to invest in full scale production. Ultimately the Hercules was renamed by its critics and today is known as the Spruce Goose, a symbol more of failure than success.

As this story illustrates, simply providing a solution isn't enough. Half of any victory requires winning the hearts, and support of others.

With this in mind, I prefer the following definition.

Execution - The discipline of doing simple things consistently and well.

As this definition suggests, effective execution involves a combination of factors beyond simply completing a task. Let's examine each word one at a time.

* * * * * *

MASTERING YOURSELF

In discussing discipline, we are *not* referring to the academic disciplines such as law, art, or science. We are also not referring to the type of discipline used to *enforce* a behavior through reward, punishment or intimidation.

The type of discipline associated with execution involves that human attribute known as self-control. It is this type of discipline that makes the act of executing a form of art. Discipline keeps emotions from driving our actions, and requires a clear mind that can concentrate on doing a few simple things consistently and well.

One area where we see this form of discipline is in our military and emergency services personnel. When facing a dangerous situation, it is the discipline developed through training which allows these individuals to first assess the situation, and respond appropriately while maintaining full control of their emotions, and decision making abilities.

It is discipline to his trade that distinguishes the master craftsman from the apprentice when crafting a flawless work.

Perfection in execution requires discipline in the form of a conscious committed to do ones very best. It requires discipline to remain engaged even when a task grow tedious or to remain clear-headed when a situation becomes chaotic.

Discipline is the fundamental individual characteristic essential for accomplishing a perfect performance, regardless of the area of endeavor in which the effort is directed.

Those who execute to their maximum potential do so by disciplining themselves in ways that prevent distractions from diminishing the effectiveness of their effort. Without discipline, the smallest mistake or flaw in one's performance can result in a devastating negative outcome.

* * * * * *

DOING IS MORE THAN TRYING

In 2014 a college football game took place between two nationally ranked teams. The home team was ahead by seven points and on the offensive side of play. On their next play, a long pass was thrown by the quarterback to a receiver who caught the ball and with a significant lead over the opposing defenders ran toward the goal line. One step before crossing the goal line, the receiver made a mental mistake, and casually released the football from his grasp in his enthusiasm to celebrate a score. Unfortunately, the ball itself hadn't crossed the goal line, and remained a playable ball. To the home crowd's dismay, an opposing team player picked up the loose ball, and returned it the entire length of the field to easily score. Instead of a fourteen point lead, the home team was now tied with a re-energized opponent. In the end, the mistake was a key factor in the home team losing the game.

As stated earlier, *doing* is the action of performing a task *until the objective has been achieved.* Finishing what you start is essential to successful execution.

Some people only attempt activities they are confident in achieving. One of the biggest obstacles to doing anything is overcoming personal doubts. Success occurs when thoughts reflect an "I can" or an "I will" attitude, instead of an "I'll try" attitude. Trying suggests it is acceptable to quit at a point short of the target objective. Doers don't quit.

The subtle attitude change from "I'll try" to "I will" is called ***will power***. Success happens for those with the ***willpower*** to overcome all obstacles and achieve the objective.

* * * * * *

SIMPLE THINGS

All of mankind's greatest achievements were the result of a few simple things coming together. We've all experienced moments where some small and seemingly insignificant thing had a major impact on an outcome.

The great pyramids of Egypt are the result of a simple process of cutting large stones, shaping them, transporting each block from the quarry to construction site, and placing them on top of one another to form a pyramid.

With respect to execution, a few simple things constitute the basis of every action we perform. In every circumstance, the most complex challenges we undertake always include a combination of a few simple things which become catalysts in improving our performance whether we realize it or not.

What are these simple things? They are a set of learned behaviors we exercise when performing any task. Fortunately, these simple behaviors can be further developed.

In the book titled Influencer, author Kerry Patterson discusses how there are always *vital behaviors* that influence outcomes.[11] His works points out that if you want to have the greatest influence on any endeavor, you need to bring about the appropriate behavior so that influence can take place.

---

[11] Influencer by Kerry Patterson, McGraw-Hill Publishing, 2008

What Mr. Patterson describes in his book as vital behaviors are in fact fundamental principles that characterize and define Eternal laws, or what some call natural laws.

Principles are sometimes called truths. They define and explain unchangeable cause and effect relationships that are true everywhere in the universe.

For example, Sir Isaac Newton identified a set of principles pertaining to motion, one being the Principle of Lift that describes how airflow causes an aircraft to fly. This principle is one of many associated with the Eternal Law of Gravity.

Performing a behavior produces a *cause* that by Eternal law always results in a specific *effect* or outcome.

Patterson's book goes on to explain that behavior is something we do, not some outcome we think about. He uses the example of weight loss.

"Many people think about losing weight, and even understand that to lose weight they need to burn more calories than they take in. That knowledge alone is not a behavior. Knowing the principle of weight loss doesn't cause the calories to burn off. To lose weight, a behavior needs to take place that results in exercising more, eating less, or both. Until that behavior occurs the desired outcome will never be realized."

Because this cause and effect relationship exists in Eternal laws, people often confuse outcomes as behaviors.

For example; managers know effective communication is critical to successful leadership. Many a CEO has called for improved communication across their organization. However, calling for better communication is akin to telling people what to achieve, without helping them do what is necessary to achieve it. Consequently the initiative fails to produce results.

Consider, what behaviors make for effective communication? Listening is a behavior that must occur for effective communication, an outcome, to occur. It makes no sense to suggest effective communication (an effect) will lead to improved listening (a cause). Rather, it is the behavior of better listening (cause) that improves communication (effect).

Understanding the distinction between knowing something verses applying the behavior to actually achieve it is a simple thing, but one most people struggle at. Properly applied, a few changes involving some simple behaviors become a catalyst to producing substantially better results.

* * * * * *

THE NEED FOR CONSISTENCY

Consistency makes an outcome more predictable. Precision and accuracy, pattern or rhythm, are words that describe characteristics of consistency.

At some time in life most of us have watched a juggler masterfully keep several objects rotating through the air. You may have tested your own skill at juggling two or three small objects. Chances are the attempt did not go well. Within just a few tosses the various objects began dropping to the ground or sailing out of reach. The challenge for a juggler is at being consistent with each toss in order to make the subsequent catch possible.

Consistency allows us to better leverage the laws of nature and exercise principles of cause and effect to maximize successful results.

The apparel industry offers a great example of the need for consistency. Consider the frustration customers would have if clothes that were supposed to be the same size were not consistent in measurement. To ensure consistency a pattern is used so each piece is cut and sewn to meet a standard.

Of course some allowance is sometimes necessary for deviations to occur due to unknown factors. The apparel industry has seen more than one pair of slacks split a seam due to a lack of stretch ability. Still to ensure a positive outcome, the goal is to keep deviations as narrow as possible.

Consistency is critical to maximizing your effectiveness when performing any action. The more predictable an outcome, the more likely it will be successful.

* * * * * *

DOING IT WELL

Quality is always a factor with respect to the final outcome of every endeavor. The old saying that anything worth doing is worth doing well is fundamental, and speaks to the very essence of every form of execution. Doing something well is the measure of the quality of the outcome of a task.

Perfection describes the highest level attainable in doing something well. With respect to execution, perfection is the target to aspire toward, but achieving perfection is often paid for with an investment of time and effort that can never be recovered and can result in missing other important opportunities.

Perfection, while desirable, is *not* essential. But then what is a reasonable measure of quality?

A number of years ago I had a department manager who was a former IBM director tasked with rescuing failing projects. At the time, our own project was running late. Our team was seeking perfection in the products quality, but the work was taking longer than expected and our window of opportunity was closing. The manager then suggested that a reasonable measure of quality means being just a little better than your competition.

The problem is we can't always know how good our competition is. Therefore the recommendation is to always do things as well as you possibly can with the time you have been allotted in order to meet or exceed your own and in some cases others expectations. If you always do your best, you will have done as well as can be expected given the environmental constraints.

In order to meet or exceed expectations, you have to establish in advance what those expectations are, and the environment they must operate within. The scuba diver whose breathing apparatus functions under water is probably not equipped to operate in the environment of outer space.

Today, one of the great flaws in many corporations annual performance review process is their failure to establish and communicate management's expectations for the quality of an employee's work well in advance of the employee's performance review. Typically, if a worker fails to meet their bosses expectations, their failure begins with the leadership that failed to properly communicate their expectations to the employee.

Establishing a standard of quality is necessary in order to know if you are performing well.

* * * * * *

The Simple Things

Behavior 1 - Awareness

Behavior 2 - Focus

Behavior 3 - Balance

Behavior 4 - Timing

Behavior 5 - Communication

Behavior 6 - Details

Behavior 7 - Precision

Behavior 8 – Attitude

Chapter One

Awareness

"If I were asked for the most important advice I could give, that which I considered to be the most useful to the men of our century, I should simply say: in the name of God, stop a moment, cease your work, and look around you." [12]

The Wasatch Mountain Range extends south from the Utah-Idaho border for about 160 miles. Millions of years ago, glaciers carved out numerous canyons along this range. On the western side of the Wasatch Range, about 30 miles south of Salt Lake City is the mouth of American

[12] Leo Tolstoy, Essays, Letters and Miscellaneous

Fork canyon. Evidence shows the canyon was populated by early native cultures, and later became a source of various minerals and timber for the pioneers that settled in the area.

A few miles up the canyon from is the Department of Interior operated Visitor and Information Center for Timpanogos Cave National Monument.

Between 1887, and 1921 three distinct caverns were discovered and rediscovered in Mt. Timpanogos by various individuals. The first of these caverns was found by a logger seeking timber on the steep slopes. The other two caverns were discovered later by visitors and family members who were hunting in the canyon.

The three caverns were subsequently connected by man-made tunnels to create a multi-cavern cave system. In addition a trail was built to make it easier for visitors to reach the cave. Today, during the summer months, the U.S. forest service provides guided tours of the cave throughout the day.

The cave's entrance is at a point approximately 1,000 feet above the canyon floor. Access requires visitors to hike up a relatively steep paved trail that originates at the Visitor and Information Center.

To preserve the caves delicate limestone features and prevent predatory wildlife from populating the cave, the natural openings have been covered so that inside the cave there is no natural light.

At some point during the tour the guide will extinguishes the interior lights, leaving everyone drenched in total darkness, and will ask that visitors restrict their speaking to a quiet whisper. Soon the only sounds are those created by visitors moving gingerly about in the blackness. One might hear occasional splashing from drops of water that over millennia have formed various limestone tubes, shields, stalactite, and stalagmite features.

Soon visitors begin to notice odors trapped within the moist but stagnant air. You can taste the minerals present in the caverns. In the silence you can not only hear the beating of your own heart, but the heartbeat of people standing near you.

Our eyes are responsible for 90% of the information we obtain, and immersed in darkness the eye's pupils dilate to their maximum. The brain, lacking its primary source of stimuli, strains for input and slowly begins to enhance the other senses. It seeks information, striving to be aware.

A*wareness* is the first behavior needed to execute effectively.

So what is awareness? Awareness is the act of assimilating that which is taking place within our environment and developing a more complete understanding of our situation.

Awareness allows us to live in the moment while anticipating future consequences, then take action to avoid, mitigate, transfer, and either minimize or maximize the impact.

When we are aware, we recognize factors that we can leverage as opposed to respond to. Awareness helps us adapt, adjust and pursue alternatives.

Without awareness, luck drives the success or failure of events. It is impossible to consciously take action relative to things we are not aware of. The greater our awareness, the more likely we are to apply that knowledge to our advantage.

Awareness also has a time factor associated with it. If you are attending a baseball game, and a player hits the ball in your direction, you want to know well in advance if it is headed toward you so you have time to react and avoid being hit in the face by the ball.

Awareness is not just a personal behavior. It is applicable in many areas of our society. Consider;

Sports teams gather information on opponents so as to be aware of their opponent's abilities in order to develop a more effective game plan.

Governments devote massive resources gathering intelligence information and analyzing it in order to be aware of global activities that can impact their citizens and society.

Businesses seek information so as to be aware of market opportunities and emerging technologies in order to gain an advantage over competitors.

For people, our awareness is an innate ability, meaning it is an ability we are born with. It is also an ability that varies within each of us. Even when an individual's ability from birth is exceptional, it is still possible to further develop this ability.

This innate ability begins in the form of our five senses, vision, touch, smell, taste, and hearing. The senses provide the information about the world around us that enables us to be aware.

Jack Canfield, once stated, "By taking the time to stop and appreciate who you are and what you've achieved – and perhaps learned through a few mistakes, stumbles and losses – you actually can enhance everything about you".[13]

* * * * * * *

SELF AND SITUATIONAL AWARENESS

When discussing awareness, the dialogue generally centers around two areas. The first is self-awareness, the second is situational awareness. Both have their place when it comes to execution.

Self-awareness deals with understanding yourself, what motivates and drives you, your attitude, morals, ideals, what you desire, your goals, and talents.

We are all different, and have different outlooks. Different things drive us, and make us happy or sad. We find pleasure in different things, different colors, different kinds of music, different styles of clothes, different scenery, and different personalities. Self-awareness is about discovering what drives you, your thought, actions, and your behaviors.

Situational awareness is about understanding and assessing the current environment, and discovering the factors driving the people or events taking place around us.

---

[13] Jack Canfield is an American author, and co-author of the Chicken Soup for the Soul series.

Through situational awareness we gather the information needed to adapt and respond. When we are aware of the situation, we can make choices that increase our own or others happiness, improve an outcome, increase opportunities, and diminish failures. In short, our execution improves.

Everyone can develop increased self and situational awareness, but this requires us making a *conscious effort*. Many people find that maintaining a personal journal helps them analyze their day, and evaluate their actions and behavior. However you choose to become more aware, start by making it a daily practice.

****

DEVELOPING AWARENESS

There are many techniques for increasing awareness.

Reflection is a technique for improving awareness. I previously mentioned the practice of keeping a journal. Maintaining a journal provides a way to look back at past experiences and learn from them. Writing things down forces us to remember the events taking place and reflect on them. It forces us to think about what took place and recognize things that in the heat of the moment were not obvious.

Reflection is best in moments of calm, rather than during intense moments of activity when emotion or adrenaline can influence actions and decisions.

That said, usually it is critical to increase our awareness of events occurring *at the moment*. It is a little late to wait to record in your journal that you were hit by a train and killed. Some things require immediate awareness. It starts by making awareness a conscious habit.

For most of us, the primary cause for a lack of awareness is simply the failure to take a moment to look around in order to be more aware of what is going on.

Consider, when you park your car, do you take a moment to note where it was parked so you can find your car later?

Do you look both ways before crossing the street, twice? Before leaving the house, do you check your appearance in the mirror; confirm that a stove was not left on, or that you haven't forgotten your wallet, checkbook, or sunglasses, etc.? Are you aware of the time? Do you consciously make a mental note where you set down your keys, purse, or wallet?

These are simple things that if neglected can result in a less than desirable outcome. The same types of awareness behaviors apply to every aspect of the things we do in business, church, community, etc.

To improve your awareness, begin by asking questions. Who is in attendance? What is the agenda? Who is in charge? What hasn't been considered? What is missing? How have conditions changed?

Of course the biggest problem isn't always about gathering information, but determining if the information has relevance. Consider that for most people, much of the daily news we hear broadcast has little if any relevance to our own lives.

Obtaining information for the sake of being informed doesn't contribute to our ability to be more effective. Libraries are filled with information that is largely irrelevant. Establishing what and when information is relevant is the challenge.

The second key practice to developing awareness involves evaluating whether the information enhances the vision or value of activities you are engage in, or if it is a distraction that prevents you from focusing on what is important.

The mind has the incredible capability to store and retain all the information it takes in, but it also filters information from our consciousness that *it has been trained* to consider irrelevant. People who live by noisy railroad tracks know that this type of filtering happens. My wife refers to it as selective hearing.

Increasing awareness requires retraining the mind to know when and what information is important, and what to filter out. One problem is that no two people share the same informational requirements. We must determine for ourselves what type of information we need.

In his stories Sir Author Conan Doyle's character known as Sherlock Holmes, was a master at discerning information present in the environment around him and subsequently categorizing, prioritizing and establishing its relevance to solving a problem. His ability to see beyond the obvious allowed Holmes to grasp the underlying facts of a situation. Holmes talent for observation set him apart from his peers.

One reason Sherlock Holmes was able to recognize clues beyond the obvious was because he acquired through personal study a wealth of information in a broad range of subjects, but not just any subject. Holmes studies topics that would facilitate investigations and help him decipher clues that criminals might inadvertently leave behind.

To Sherlock Holmes, a few bits of tobacco at a crime scene offered more than the obvious fact someone had been smoking. His studies included categorizing characteristics of various tobaccos, allowing him to identify any type of tobacco he encounters. This potentially leads him to a unique brand of cigar. He also developed a list of tobacco sellers, including which brands were available at the various shops. By obtaining a list of the customers who purchase a specific tobacco brand, Holmes was able to create a short list of suspects.

Many of today's leading corporations are engaged in a similar activity know as data mining. Their objective it to know as much as possible about consumers, shopping trends, fashion styles, etc. so they can target their marketing efforts in a more effective manner.

Improving our awareness requires cultivating a broad knowledge of many subject areas. It is easier to appreciate art if you know something about art. People who study cars are more likely to appreciate the features or style of different models. This increased awareness is benefited by developing a more in-depth knowledge of those subjects that could have a direct or indirect impact on the activities you engage in.

The point is that the brain, with training has the capability to significantly increase its awareness of the constantly changing environment we live in. Those who learn to develop a behavior of increasing awareness will significantly improve their effectiveness when executing.

Lastly, we have all experienced that mental state called day dreaming. When we day dream, our state of awareness to the things taking place around us diminishes. We see things differently, or fail to hear or understand what others are saying. When we day dream we become unaware. Some people get so addicted to this state of mindless thinking that they seek this state by utilizing alcohol or mind influencing drugs that alter their reality.

If not monitored, this lack of conscious attention trains the mind to treat everything as unimportant.

In stark contrast, in life and death situations, people have stated that during that brief intense period of time when life hung in the balance, the world around them seems to be in slow motion. The extreme intensity of the moment causes the mind to accelerate its activity to a point that these individuals became aware of even minute details involving everything taking place around them. The experience is described as seeing life flash before your eyes.

This happens when the brain is in a heightened level of activity. Our normal cognitive mind is so busy compared to its normal activity that our awareness of things appears to move slower than they in fact are.

We sometimes experience this when travelling at faster than normal speeds for long periods of time. Our mind become accustom to processing the increased amount of information passing by. However, when subsequently slowing down the mind need to readjust. Deceleration can make normally high speeds seem incredibly slow since the mind is expecting information at the higher rate.

The brain is one of the primary consumers of energy in the body. During very intense moments, the mind consumes even more energy in the form of glucose, and over an extended duration, it can leave a person physically exhausted. It is therefore important to take a break once in a while to allow the body time to refuel from stored energy.

Continuous improvement is an often discussed topic in the business world. It is interesting to consider, but the first step toward implementing improvements requires awareness of where ones performance is currently at. This requires obtaining some form of metric.

Metrics can help establish a baseline upon which to measure improvement. Awareness occurs by analyzing the metrics to achieve greater understanding of how execution of an activity might be improved.

To summarize, making a conscious effort to be more aware is a simply thing that only requires some discipline to be more effective.

Chapter Two

Focus

"Whenever you want to achieve something, keep your eyes open, concentrate and make sure you know exactly what it is you want. No one can hit their target with their eyes closed." [14]

The retina of the human eye contains two types of photoreceptors, rods and cones. According to experts in human anatomy, the rods are more numerous in the amount of approximately 120 million. The rods are more sensitive than the cones and therefore generate more impulses to the brain. However, the rods are not sensitive to color.

---

[14] Paula Coelho, The Devil and Miss Prym

Cones provide the eye's color sensitivity. In comparison, to the rods, the eye has relatively few cones, a mere six to seven million.

To better appreciate the level of concentration and proximity of these receptors consider that today's high definition televisions use approximately two million pixels dispersed across a 46 inch diagonal monitor.

The cones in the eye are largely concentrated at the back of the eye within an area known as the Macula. At the center of the Macula is the "Fovea Centralis" an entirely rod-free area comprised entirely of very thin, densely packed cones. These highly concentrated cones gather light equivalent to very high resolution images for the brain to process.

While the combination of rods and cones in the human eye are able to detect motion in a 200 degree field we call peripheral vision, the portion of an image upon which we *focus* our attention is limited to the Fovea Centralis. This small region limits the acute vision angle to about 15 degrees.

In order to focus on objects of special interest, we unconsciously position our head and eyes so that the projected image of items of interest falls on this dense set of cones in the Fovea Centralis.

You can experience this by picking two objects in the room about three feet away from you, and at least two feet apart, each with details that require that you concentrate in order to see them clearly.

Without turning your head or moving your eyes, see if you can identify details of the second object while still looking at the details of the first item. Unless you are someone exceptional, you will not be able to. Next try moving your eyes back and forth between the two objects as quickly as you can, ensuring before each move that you clearly see the detail of each object, as opposed to simply shifting back and forth and creating a visual blur.

You will discover that it requires a moment; a fraction of a second perhaps, for your eyes to move and stabilize on the object in order to process its image. For that brief moment, your mental capabilities align to focus on the object.

The second behavior of effective execution is the ability to *focus* your mental capabilities. Focus is the art of not allowing attention to wander, but to concentrate on the task.

While the part of the brain that deals with vision is located at the back of the head, the area of the brain that deals with making cognitive choices involving priorities, avoiding distractions and managing information conflicts is located just behind the forehead along a strip of neurons in your prefrontal cortex. This is the administrative part of the brain.

Dan Goleman writes that, "Focus is the hidden ingredient in excellence, hidden because we typically don't notice it. But lacking focus we are more likely to falter at whatever we do. A test of how concentrated college athletes are, for instance, predicts their sports performance the following semester. Studies show that a wandering mind punches holes in students' comprehension of what they study." [15]

When applied to execution, focus is a mental activity that applies to all of your senses, and a behavior that through training can be improved.

In the previous section on awareness, a key objective was to acquire a broad view of the situation in order to become aware of the bigger picture. Armed with information, the objective now is to remove distractions and make adjustments that will allow you to focus on achieving the objective.

Consider a football quarterback attempting to pass the ball to a team mate. Awareness requires knowing where the intended receiver is on the playing field and identifying any threats from opposing players. Being aware of the current situation, he next *focuses* on throwing the ball to a location where only the intended receiver can catch it.

---

[15] The Brain & Emotional Intelligence, 7 Oct., 2013, Dan Goleman, Ph.D.

The late Steve Jobs who helped make Apple the most valuable company in the world once said that "focus isn't about deciding what to do, but deciding what not to do". The distinction is critical! Too often we allow distractions to move our focus away from the objectives.

Focus requires consciously reprioritizing information to prevent distractions from getting in the way, and utilizing information to execute as effectively as possible.

Marianne Downing an Executive Consultant wrote an article that was posted on the internet entitled, "Lessons from Houdini – Our Great Escape".

The article explains that when Houdini invited people onto the stage to inspect locks, chains, strait-jackets, and other devices, it was to set the audiences expectations that escape was virtually impossible. The reality of course was that Houdini already had devised his escape, and was focused on executing the illusion. The locks and chains were simply obstacles introduced to make the effort seem impossible.

Focused on the obstacles, Houdini's audience would then anticipate what to them appeared to be the logical outcome.

It is human nature to focus on the obstacles, and thereby fail to explore options or examine alternate solutions to challenges. Houdini focused on the solution, and as a result the seemingly impossible obstacles he introduced to distract the audience were easily overcome.

Most people in the world are obsessed with the idea that there is only one solution to a problem, and that the solution must be politically correct, or must not be offensive to people who might have a different view. That type of thinking is an obstacle.

Many individuals, business leaders, and politicians, have difficulty seeing any solution to a problem or issue they personally did not devise or contribute toward its creation. These people will feel threatened by alternate views or suggestions fearing that someone else's proposed approach might somehow diminish their own personal standing. They lose their focus on the original objective, and will move it to protecting their position until the threat is eliminated. They will remain firm, despite knowing they may have the weaker solution.

Brian Tracy has stated, "the key to success is to focus our conscious mind on things we desire not things we fear".[16]

****

THE MULTI TASKING MYTH

In the business world it is a common expectation that employees multi-task. Multi-tasking describes the effort of performing two or more tasks at the same time. It has come to be considered essential in most professions.

Multi-tasking has two flavors;

1) Concurrent / Parallel Tasking.
2) Serial Shift Tasking.

Concurrent Tasking consists in doing two or more activities *simultaneously* over a period of time. It typically takes place when the activities;

1) Are simple, similar, and require minimal mental focus.
2) Can use subconscious mind to perform tasks while the primary task is performed by the conscious mind.
3) Involve data with only a short duration of relevancy.

Examples include such things as driving a car while listening to a radio or engaging in conversation, riding an exercise bike while listening to music or watching TV, playing the piano or guitar while singing a song.

---

[16] Brian Tracy is a self-development speaker, author, and business coach.

Serial Shift Tasking involves *shifting* ones mental focus back and forth between two or more activities of a serial nature over a period of time. It occurs when;

1) Work is complex with many discrete activities taking place that require a lengthy time period to complete, but usually are accomplished in multiple short bursts.
2) Each task requires a high level of concentration.
3) Includes interruptions or delays that require attention which temporarily shift ones focus.

An example might be answering the phone while preparing a large meal in the kitchen. The call diverts attention away from the meal preparation to responding to the caller's needs, and might require temporarily moving to a different location to find and communicate some specific information, before ending the call and returning back to preparing the meal.

Let's look at each of these one at a time.

The first question to ask is, is concurrent tasking really possible? The answer is, yes, but it is not effective.

Although the brain controls all our actions, many actions are delegated to the subconscious mind and overall nervous system of the body like scratching an itch, climbing stairs, or throwing a ball. Concurrent processing leverages our ability to relegate simple or familiar activities to the subconscious mind, thereby allowing us to do multiple tasks concurrently.

The challenge occurs when trying to *consciously* do multiple things concurrently that require us to focus. It is at this time that concurrent tasking breaks down, or forces a switch to using serial shift tasking.

Researchers have discovered that what restricts our ability to do concurrent tasking effectively is our short term memory capacity.

Short term memory is used when the information being processed is relevant for only a short period of time, typically less than 20 seconds.

When information must be retained longer than about 20 seconds it is transferred to long-term memory, or somehow refreshed to make it current.

An example might be a situation of being introduced to someone you've never met. If you expect to interact with the individual in the future, you make a mental note to remember the name in your long term memory, or you might help refresh your short term memory by calling the person by their name, e.g. Happy to meet you Mr. Jones, then regularly using the name in your conversation.

When we try to do too many things concurrently, short term memory overflows forcing information quickly into long term memory. This can result in gaps in the information being received while the older information is stored or refreshed to keep it relevant.

When the mind struggles with too many rapidly changing activities, these gaps confuse the logic creating uncertainty and confusion, leading to responses like; "I'm sorry, what were you saying?"

When the mind is unable to refresh information that has been lost, the mind may seek to fill the gap from random bits and pieces of latent data. This "fill–the-gap" information is what the mind assumed was occurring. It is thoughts that can be totally inaccurate, and result in the making of poor decisions. Witnesses to crimes will occasionally fill gaps in their memories recollection using random information about the scene in an effort to explain a detail they forgot or missed some segment of while attempting to do some other urgent task.

Unlike concurrent tasking, serial shift tasking depends almost entirely on the conscious mind.

When an individual task is complex requiring considerable mental processing, our brain shifts into serial tasking mode. When this switchover occurs, we stop trying to do concurrent processing and mentally focus on doing just one task. The focus on this one task continues until something interrupts the thought process creating, a mental distraction that shifts our focus to a different activity. Although we are only focused on a single task at the moment, multi-tasking is considered to be occurring while our attention focuses back and forth between the multiple tasks.

When interrupted the mind temporarily switches focus in order to respond to the interruption. This can give the impression of doing two tasks simultaneously, but in fact only a single task is still actually being focused on. The original task is temporarily set aside, and a temporary administrative task created to keep track of the paused activity while focus changes to deal with the interruption.

A common assumption with respect to serial shift tasking is that it results in a more efficient outcome. The premise is that when engaging in two or more activities, our time is better utilized, thereby maximizing our work output. Surprisingly, research indicates this is true only some of the time.

Research by Alessandro Acquisti, a professor of information technology, and psychologist Eyal Peer at Carnegie Mellon Human Computer Interaction Lab conducted experiments on multi-tasking. The experiment included individuals in three groups; the control group (no interruptions), an interrupted group (two interruptions), and an on-high alert group. This third group was interrupted once, and told to expect a second interruption that didn't occur.

In the study, multi-tasking had a 20% reduction in efficiency in completing the assignment. Repeated tests saw some improvement, but the cause for improvement requires additional study. When the task being interrupted is especially complex, it was found that returning back to a fully productive state after only a single simple interruption can require as long as 25 minutes.

Statistically women seem better at this type of multi-tasking than men. When men engage in multi-tasking their effectiveness diminishes by as much as 15%. By comparison, women diminished by only 5%.

Why is this?

It seems that women are better at breaking down work into more, short or simpler tasks that when completed can be mentally cross-off, leaving less to administrate. Men fail to break work down to the same level, and therefore manage fewer but slightly more complex activities that require more time to complete, and therefore more effort to administrate.

Either way, the mind consumes a percentage of processing cycles to manage multiple activities and the shift in mental focus that is required.

Doug Merrill, a contributor at Forbes explained this in an article he wrote titled, "Why Multi-tasking doesn't work".[17]

He states, "When you're trying to accomplish two dis-similar tasks, each one requiring some level of consideration and attention, multitasking falls apart. Your brain just can't take in and process multiple streams of relatively dis-similar information and encode them fully into short-term memory."

Multi-tasking forces us to expend additional effort to manage multiple activities. The effort becomes another task that consumes processing cycles and clouds focus. Ultimately overall efficiency diminishes.

The bottom line is that humans don't multi-task very well.

Joshua Rubinstein, Ph.D., of the Federal Aviation Administration, along with David Meyer, Ph.D., and Jeffrey Evans, Ph.D., both at the University of Michigan, describe their research into multi-tasking in a report published back in August of 2001.[18] Their report states:

"... measurements revealed that for all types of tasks, subjects lost time when they had to switch from one task to another, and time costs increased with the complexity of the tasks, so it took significantly longer to (mentally) switch between more complex tasks. Time costs also were

---

[17] 8/17/2012 Forbes http://www.forbes.com/sites/douglasmerrill/2012/08/17/why-multitasking-doesnt-work/

[18]` *Journal of Experimental Psychology: Human Perception and Performance Vol 27(4,* American Psychological Association (APA)

greater when subjects switched to tasks that were relatively unfamiliar. They got up to speed faster when they switched to tasks they knew better".

We see the impact of this constantly in business where a common practice is to assign additional work to an individual, until the effort consumes more time and attention than the individual has available. The result is an ultimate failure to execute.

Doctors Rubinstein, Meyer, and Evans report, the challenge to multi-task increases significantly when activities increase in complexity or differ in terms of familiarity

Multi-tasking erodes focus decreasing the effectiveness of execution. The same challenges apply to every form of execution.

As a project manager I often had teams filled with individuals assigned to work on multiple projects across the organization. Many of these people were allocated to spend only 20% of their time on my project, effectively just one day a week.

Now so far as my own project went, they would attend our weekly one hour communication meeting, a daily fifteen minute stand-up meeting for status and planning, and also participate in various project related design presentations. Ultimately they ended up with less than a half day a week to perform the specific work activities they were assigned to move the project forward. The half day a week of general overhead associated with being part of the team, and which was required to administer the project consumed most of their limited allocation of time. Their need to work on other projects constrained their effort. Assuming this pattern was true of the other projects they were assigned to, these people might only be productive across the organization no more than 50% of the week. If the practice were applied to all the other employees, it could be determined that all projects were taking twice as long to complete, cost twice the budgeted amount, or that the company needed to double the staff.

Another reason multi-tasking is a challenge is that our brain is already subconsciously engaged doing multiple tasks.

Besides absorbing input from our five senses and filtering out irrelevant content, our brain is controlling our actions, directing our thoughts, gathering previously stored information, searching, matching, visualizing, contemplating, interpreting and evaluating thousands of bits of information.

The more we try to do simultaneously, the more likely the mind will become confused and mix signals.

****

THE RULE OF THREE

Admittedly, life requires some amount of multi-tasking. There are times when multi-tasking cannot be avoided. The question then becomes how many tasks can be managed concurrently before performance degrades.

The short answer is that performance degrades immediately when attempting to do more than a single task. However, on average, it seems people can engage in about three activities before performance becomes totally unsatisfactory.

The rule of three can easily be observed when people are asked to demonstrate their juggling skills. As you know, juggling is a hand and eye coordinating skill that uses the common everyday actions of reaching for a tossed object with one hand, catching the object, and tossing that object back into the air. It introduces these three actions with a rhythmic pattern. The practiced individual learns to maintain the rhythmic task of catching and tossing accurately from the same location so as to minimize the time and effort needed to randomly reach about for the juggled objects.

Most people can juggle two objects with one hand without much difficulty and with practice become adept juggling three objects of similar size and shape using two hands. The problem occurs when asked to juggle four objects, or objects that are substantially dis-similar. Extending one talent to this next level requires a major investment in time to practice.

Imagine trying to play three sports, tennis, basketball, and golf simultaneously. All three are similar in the sense that they are all competitive activities, they each have unique elements in terms of the playing field, type of ball, number of opposing players, style of play, etc. The unique elements with respect to the different sports create constraints that limit the ability to compete in all three simultaneously. While a person might be exceptionally talented in all three of these sports, attempting to play all three simultaneously would be impossible to do, let alone do well. The same can be said of other types of activities we are asked to take upon us.

Unfortunately we are often put in situations that require us to multi-task dis-similar efforts. To please others we take on these additional tasks until they exceed our ability to effectively focus. The solution is learning to say “No”.

When it comes to execution, even the most accomplished professionals have difficulty juggling more than three dis-similar tasks concurrently. The Rule of Three means limiting yourself to no more than three simultaneous tasks, fewer if possible.

The best approach is to whenever possible focus on doing just one thing consistently and well until it is completed.

Focus is a relatively simple behavior to develop. The discipline is in not allowing you to start a second activity until you either set the current task aside for later, or fully complete it before starting a new task.

* * * * * * *

Chapter Three

Balance

"The major work of the world is not done by geniuses. It is done by ordinary people, with balance in their lives, who have learned to work in an extraordinary manner." [19]

Since ancient times Balance Scales have been used to compare the weight or mass of two objects. Balance Scales in the traditional form consists of a beam centered on a pivotal fulcrum creating horizontal levers of equal length arms. From these arm is suspended a pan, called a *scale* or *scale pan*, hence the plural term "scales" for the entire instrument. To

[19] Gordon B Hinckley

ensure its operation is friction free, the fulcrum has a knife edge pivot to rest on.

Because of its sensitivity to variations, the balance scale is one of the most accurate measuring technologies ever invented. To operate it, an object of unknown mass is placed in one pan to be weighed. Standard weights of known mass are then added to the other pan until the beam is as close to equilibrium as possible.

When it comes to execution, maintaining equilibrium or balance can be critical to success. To function effectively requires establishing and maintaining balance in the five areas of human health and wellbeing. These are your; physical, mental, emotional, social, and spiritual health.

Balance is the third behavior of effective execution.

Balance itself is not a behavior, but is the result of choices we make with regard to every decision we are faced with. Making decisions is a behavior and a simple thing if you choose wisely. Problems occur when poor decisions are made that result in negative consequences.

THE CASE FOR BALANCE

Shortly after we are born we begin the struggle of learning to walk. As parents we watch our children first learn to stand by grasping hold of a table leg or chair to find stability as they rise to stand on their feet. As they gain confidence and step away from the chair they will swerve a little back and forth, over compensate, and fall back or tumble forward. Through persistence there comes a day when their effort pays off and we see them toddle across the room, excited at their increased mobility. This is only one aspect of balance.

As we get older we develop in other behavior areas that involve finding equilibrium such as balancing personal needs with wants, how and where we spend our time, making smart choices in the food we eat, budgeting financial expenditures against income, etc.....

When we find ourselves out of equilibrium it is difficult to perform well. Being out of balance in one area can also influence other areas. It is much more difficult for an athlete who is not in a balanced state of equilibrium to throw a pass, shoot a ball, or successfully place a kick. Consider also how difficult it can be to concentrate on work related activities when your health is out of balance. When our personal finances are out of balance, purchases can be restricted or delayed. Delays can result in missing opportunities or force us to take risks that create imbalance in other areas.

In the area of competitive sports we often hear about the need for both a balanced offense and defense. Many sports use strategies designed to keep an opponent off-balance. It is critical for athletes to maintain equilibrium when performing their sport.

In business balance is essential. Companies must balance expenditures against revenue. To keep equipment operational there must be balance between production and downtime for maintenance. Also a business can't bow to one client without balancing the needs of other clients.

Effective communicators must balance listening with speaking. Educators must balance their own learning to remain informed with the time spent teaching others. Researchers must balance study with recording findings.

In social situations relationships can become strained if one person demands attention and validation from others without reciprocating. Both people in relationships need to feel loved, appreciated, and valued. When the emotional bank account is not balanced, the relationship suffers.

Relative to our physical well-being, physicians have encouraged balancing the calories we consume, with physical activity to maintain a healthy lifestyle.

In the pursuit of education some people struggle to balance academic studies with practical experience. Theoretical knowledge needs to be balanced with real world experience.

Time spent on a career must be balanced with family and personal interests. Time spent with children must be balanced with the time spent with a spouse. Time spent on fun activities and entertainment must be balanced with meeting commitments and responsibilities.

It is critical to establish balance and maintain it throughout. A slip from equilibrium can be very difficult to restore.

****

ACHIEVING BALANCE

Most practices for staying balanced seem new, but many actually have their origin in ancient traditions that are being re-packaged or adapted to modern times. Our progenitors faced the same types of challenges we face and like us battled to overcome them. Rather than repeat mistakes, we can leverage ideas discovered by those who preceded us. That means not only listening to our parents, but gaining insight from history itself.

First of all, "Balance is not something you find. It is something you create".

The late Steven Covey discussed balancing priorities between matters that are both important and urgent as a habit he titled "Putting First Things First". [20]

The ancient Romans recognized the need for checks and balance in their form of government. These included limiting the duration of time people served in a position of power, or creating a separation of powers. Following this model has helped the United States avoid the tyrannical practices found in some other forms of government.

Centuries ago the Chinese introduced the concept of Yin and Yang to balance opposites such as; dark-light, male-female, or old-young.

---

[20] The Seven Habit of Highly Effective people, by Steven Covey, Covey Leadership Training Center, 1996

In ancient Egypt, wisdom was regarded as something people acquired as a result of obeying the "natural" laws that regulated balance in life.

In Celtic culture the five-fold symbol is thought by some to represent a *balance* in human nature.

While precedence is usually given to those things that are important and urgent, to achieve balance it is critical that people occasionally revisit those things that are seemingly unimportant or not urgent because priorities change. For example, a visit to the dentist may not be urgent or important at this moment, but existing tooth decay left untreated could have painful consequences if ignored too long.

Some people believe that to enjoy life to its fullest means living without boundaries or constraints, and pushing limits. Unfortunately, most of these people later regret throwing caution to the wind. It may be from the abuse of drugs, engaging in extreme sports, aggressive investments, a promiscuous lifestyle, etc.

Achieving balance requires the discipline to set boundaries in order to avoid excesses that if exceeded result in a negative outcomes. Of course as your abilities increase, boundaries should be expanded to permit personal growth, but this is accomplished by exercising discipline to establish appropriate boundaries.

Balance requires the courage to make wise but difficult choices. It is a fool and a coward who makes dumb choices without regard to consequences. Achieving balance requires taking control of your life rather than allowing life to control you. It means not only learning to say "no" when placed in a compromising situation, but being strong enough to say it repeatedly and forcefully when pressed upon by others.

More effective execution will be your reward for making a balanced approach part of your activities.

* * * * * * *

Chapter Four

Timing

"Patience is power.
Patience is not an absence of action;
rather it is timing,
it waits on the right time to act
for the right principles and in the right way." [21]

The shortest duration of time considered theoretically possible to measure is known as Planck Time. Planck time is the theoretical amount

---

[21] Fulton J Sheen

of time required for a single proton traveling at the speed of light to travel one Planck length.

A Planck length is about 10^{-20} times the diameter of a proton.

Planck time is 10^{-43} seconds. That is the numeral 1 to the right of the decimal point, and being separated by 42 zeroes or 0.0000000000 000000000000000000000000000000001.

Bottom line, a Planck length is exceedingly tiny and considered the shortest possible distance. To better picture this, it would be impossible to detect any separation between two points, A and B that are less than one Planck length apart. Points A and B may as well be the same point.

Needless to say, we lack any instrument remotely capable of measuring a unit of time or distance this small. So for argument sake, let's agree that based on what we understand today, Planck Time is the smallest unit by which time ticks.

Considering this, it becomes apparent that time ticks at an incredible high rate that makes it seem continuous.

With respect to execution, the duration to complete an activity is not the only element involving time. A more critical aspect of time involves the behaviors for coordinating multiple activities to maximize the positive outcome. This type of coordination is referred to as timing.

Timing is the fourth behavior of execution, and addresses the aspect of efficiency as well as effectiveness.

Some argue that the time required to perform a task should not be a factor in determining successful execution, but most things cannot wait forever to be completed. This means that timing is an essential component of efficient execution. Because of the global nature of our society and efficiencies achieved using advanced technology, timing now influences our level of success more today than any point in human history

Archeologists have discovered that ancient civilizations devised rudimentary tools for marking the time within a day. The sun-dial tracked time based on the movement of the sun. The sand glass established an interval based on the flow of grains of sand through the neck connecting two glass bulbs.

Traditionally society has measured time according to various re-occurring observable events in nature, some of which depend upon the perspective of the observer such as;

- Year – Approximate time required for the earth to make one rotation of the sun.
- Month – Time needed to complete a lunar cycle.
- Day – The time for Earth to rotate once on its axis.
- Hour- 15 degree rotation of the Earth.

Fairly modern clocks are built using spring driven mechanisms or electric pulses accurate to within fractions of a second. The most accurate atomic mechanisms probe for microwave signals emitted when electrons in atoms change energy levels.[22]

Marking time is one thing, but it is the timing of our actions that facilitates the successful execution of a task. When the timing is off, execution fails independent of the time of day. Precise timing is a critical element of execution. A tiny fraction of a second is often all that separates contestants from 1st and 2nd place when competing against one another.

In sports where players on a team pass a ball back and forth, the timing of each exchange is critical to ensure the transfer is successful. Kicking or throwing a ball to a team mate has to be accurate and precise to avoid the ball being intercepted.

People in the entertainment industry will tell you that a major element in the success of a performance depends upon timing. Knowing when to pronounce a line is as important as the words of the line being

---

[22] Using an atomic clock, one second is the duration of 9,192,631,770 cycles of radiation released when electrons transition between energy levels of the caesium-133 atom.

spoken. Timing allows the audience to build their anticipation and be a little more intense when the line is delivered.

In business, timing factors into delivering a product while the market's window of opportunity is open. A product delivered too early may lack the features the market is seeking, whereas a product delivered too late may lose the opportunity to capture the market and be left to gather the scraps.

A gasoline engine requires each component's timing be properly adjusted to ensure smooth optimum performance. If the timing is off, too much fuel may be consumed, or too little power generated.

Timing is a unique element and behavior specific to each type of execution. It is therefore something that is developed through research and discovery. Strive to discover ways to improve execution by perfecting those elements of execution associated with timing.

* * * * * * *

THE TIME MANAGEMENT MYTH

Time management is often mentioned as necessary to execute effectively. The truth is we can't manage time, only what we do with the time we are given.

Most people confuse time management with clock management. As just explained, time ticks along at an impossibly fast speed. Time cannot be stopped, or turned back, whereas clocks can be controlled. We can start or stop a clock, reset the time it displays, and alter the speed it advances.

While we cannot manage time we can manage the activities we engage in during a period of time. How is this done?

Begin by eliminating distractions. Turn off your phone, lock the door, avoid checking email, and find a quiet area. Distractions consume a huge percentage of time by drawing attention, our focus, away from the task.

Limit text messaging and email activity to just 2-3 times a day. Keep email to one short paragraph of no more than five sentences. If you receive two responses to a text or email, pick up the phone or schedule a time to talk.

Avoid excessive searching on the internet for worthless information, or spending time playing games online, watching television, or engaging in other types of mind-numbing activities that do not require your full attention and focus.

Avoid multi-tasking. Focus on one thing at a time. Multi-tasking doesn't reduce the amount of work or the time involved. It adds more work and more time due to the inefficiencies created in order to manage multiple tasks.

Defend your agenda by not allowing other people to dictate your work activities. Of course you need to be responsive when receiving direction from your leadership, but you need to avoid taking on work that others are responsible for, or allowing others people to distract you with their agenda.

* * * * * * *

REFUEL THE MIND

Every task requires some element of time to complete, whether it is the time to produce a report, the number of minutes in an athletic competition, or the time required to run a race. We have all experienced a situation where the allocated time begins to run short. With time expiring, the level of activity increases in order to finish or maximize our output before time expires. Question: Is this a good thing?

Modern computers use microscopic devices called transistors to perform calculations. These transistors are made from semi-conductive materials found in nature that can change its state to conduct electricity under specific conditions. Each change releases energy in the form of heat. Modern computer processors have millions of these tiny devices.

When performing a lot of calculations, both the energy used and heat released increase to the point a fan is required to cool the computer's processor. If the heat gets too high, the hot circuits will begin to produce mistakes.

The human brain operates in a similar manner. Chemicals in the brain burn oxygen and glucose for energy every time a neuron transmitter fires.

Studies have shown that we remain most effective when mental activities are no more than sixty to ninety minutes in length. What most people don't realize is that the brain is a major consumer of glucose. When an activity is mentally intense for long durations, the normal level of blood glucose drops significantly leaving us feeling burned out, tired, and less alert. When blood glucose levels are low, the brain lacks sufficient fuel to perform at peak levels, and we start to make mental mistakes, or mentally nod-off.

If we are forced to push those limits through intense mental processing, we often consume the reserve glucose stored in our liver. Left unchecked, this creates a downward spiral until fatigue finally over takes us and we begin to doze-off and fall asleep from exhaustion.

Many people deal with fatigue by consuming sugary snacks or drinks containing caffeine seeking a momentary pick-up. Ask yourself; was it the caffeine, or the sugar in the drink that helped?

Chances are it was the spike in sugar that provides a temporary mental boost due to the glucose produced which the brain needed for fuel. Caffeine will help keep you awake, but it won't keep a fatigued mind alert.

Taking a short break every couple of hours will both lower the brain's activity level allowing the body time to replenish blood glucose back to normal levels.

Of course too much sugar can be detrimental as well. Instead of a soda, drink a glass of cold water. Take a brisk walk to stimulate your metabolism. Eat a snack that will digest slowly, and if possible, take a nap. This gives your body a chance to refuel using energy stored as fat. It's a great way to diet.

Taking time to refuel is a critical element of executing at the peak of effectiveness. Remember, being productive isn't just about completing a lot of work quickly, but doing so in a manner that the work performed is done well.

****

Chapter Five

Communication

"Wise men speak because they have something to say. Fools speak because they have to say something." [23]

Swallows and Amazons is the first book in a series by English author Arthur Ransome. The books were first published in 1930, and comprise stories of the play and outdoor adventures of two families of children.

The Walker children named John, Susan, Titty and Roger are on school holidays and staying at a farm on an island surrounded in the Lake District of England.

---

[23] Plato

While sailing on the lake, they meet the Blackett children Nancy and Peggy who live in a house nearby. Besides sailing, their activities include camping, fishing, exploration and a little piracy.

In their adventures, the children join forces against the Blacketts' uncle James Turner whom they call "Captain Flint". Uncle James has become less friendly by withdrawing from the company of the children in an attempt to write his memoirs.

Separated by the lake, the children utilize a form of communication that involves semaphore flags. In this form of communication, different positions of the flags represent letters of the alphabet. By moving the flags, from one position to the next, messages can be silently transmitted and received.

Communication is the fifth behavior of execution.

Few people would question the need for efficient and effective communication as a key to executing successfully. For this reason, many works of literature on the topic espouse different practices and principles for improving communication.

There are many ways communication occurs, and many methods for exchanging information in efficient and effective ways.

For instance, light has been used in many ways to communicate. as it can be seen across great distances, particularly at night. One need only look at the stars.

An earlier method for sending a message a long distance involved the use of fire. Centuries ago soldiers along the Great Wall of Chine used fire signals to send messages nearly 500 miles in just a few hours. The technique was both efficient and effective.

A similar method involves the use of flashes of light from a mirror or some other reflective device.

Native Americans are well known for using smoke signals as a method of communicating during the day. The advantage was that the receiver could see the message without their exact location needing to be revealed. Even today, a smoke signal is used to communicate the selection of a new Pope.

Most Americans are familiar with the story of the mid-night ride of Paul Revere. Paul was tasked with warning townships of the advance of British soldiers, but needed to know the route the soldiers would be taking. He was notified as to that route by lamps displayed from a church tower. The story say; one lamp if by land, two if by sea.

Spies communicate by the use of specially agreed upon signals such as a curtain being open or closed, a chalk mark on a wall, or a light being left on or off.

Deaf individuals utilize sign language where different hand gestures and movements have specific meaning. Blind people use raised bumps on paper known as braille to read letters and words.

For years people have written letters sent by mail. For a short period of time, the Pony Express was used to carry mail across the western portion of the United States before the telegraph became a faster alternative.

At one time people felt starved for news. Printed publications made information on a wide range of topics accessible to almost everyone at affordable rates. Newspapers and other publications have for years made it possible to share information on activities taking place within hours or days of their occurring.

Where once timely communication was a challenge, in our world today communication is an almost instantaneous event. Today electronic mail and instant messaging have become the more common means of communicating.

WINDOWS AND CLOAKS

The challenge today is as much about how information is communicated as it is about the content, and timing.

The speed of which communication occurs is only one factor in the efficiency and effectiveness of execution.

Transparency is a word used to describe the open and frankness by which information is communicated. While we think of a window as transparent, we are all aware of ways that clear glass can be made more opaque, or foggy. Call it dirt, mineral deposits, or whatever you want. Often, what we are told or perceive as being transparent is not crystal clear. Real effective execution requires communication be crystal clear between all parties.

Of course there are times when communication must purposely be obscured. Life is filled with cloak and dagger moments where sensitive information must be hidden, encoded or encrypted to make it difficult for someone not intended as the recipient to obtain the message. In these situations, it is critical that the encrypted information also be easily deciphered by the intended recipient.

In some situations, it is illegal to withhold information. For example; financial instruments associated with public companies requires full disclosure to all interested parties of a company's financial health. In these cases there are rules to ensure whatever is being communicated is done in a manner that everyone receives the same information in an accurate and timely manner.

In some cases, information may not be withheld, but is buried in an ocean of information for the express purpose of making it difficult to identify and understand.

Deceptive communication is similarly done thru various practices, such as using words in ways that do not convey any meaningful information. Many politicians are experts in this form of expression, using terms or flowery phrases that say nothing actually relevant. It is up to the listener to recognize this is occurring.

Methods of communicating include types of literature such as books, magazines, briefs, specifications, or designs. It includes drawings, pictures, photographs, paintings, and other forms of expression such as music, or poetry.

Communication also occurs in the type of clothes people wear, their mannerism, and the culture they express. We recognize healthcare people by the type or color of scrubs worn in healthcare settings. We identify members of the clergy, police officers, firemen, judges, soldiers, and dozens of other professionals by their uniform. Uniforms communicate a person's commitment to the service they perform, and the level of professionalism they seek to achieve.

Much is said today of our casual lifestyle. That lifestyle also communicates a casual approach to how we execute. To some, a casual lifestyle suggests a lack of commitment to planning, punctuality, precision, presentation, process, or even perspiration. How a person dresses communicates a great deal about them.

Often woman will wear a low cut top that reveals their cleavage, but will then complain that men and other women are constantly looking at their chest and not their face. The selection of clothing we wear sends a message to the people around us, but it isn't always the message that was intended to be sent.

As you can see, communication is accomplished through a wide range of simple behaviors or practices that often speak louder than our voice and silently scream messages that if we heard them would make us stop and question our actions.

****

IMPROVING THE MESSAGE

What are those simple things that help improve communication in ways that make our execution more effective? Here is a list of some thinks that if done as part of your communication will make the message and therefore your execution more effective.

Be precise and to the point. If some background information is needed, ok, but be brief. People often tune out if the point isn't made quickly.

Listen more than you talk. If you understand others, you are in a better position to respond in a meaningful way.

Be a good story teller. All life is a story, and people love a good story.

Use words people understand and that are appropriate for the audience. Adults respect people with an adult vocabulary but who can explain things in ways a child can understand.

Be honest. Lies require additional lies to hide them, and when a lie is discovered it can costs honor, trust, and have dozens of negative ramifications.

Don't be in a hurry. More time is wasted repeating a message that wasn't properly thought through or clearly expressed. People frequently will leave a voice message and include their phone number expecting a call back, but when leaving the number speak in a mumbled manner and so fast that the digits are not comprehendible.

Know your audience. Adjust your style to match the listener without compromising the message content. People at a medical convention might understand a doctor's terminology which is often based on Latin, but probably not a group of High School students. For them it may as well be Greek.

When possible, practice how you will be communicating your ideas so you come to understand for yourself what you are attempting to tell others. What you communicate may be clear in your mind because you know the context of what you are describing, but your listener may not share that understanding. You may need to provide some context.

Many times people speak off a set of notes, and when facing an audience find it difficult to organize their thoughts and words into clear concise sentences.

Avoid getting stuck filling gaps with fillers words and phrases like; umm, you know, and ah, …., you get the point.

* * * * * * *

Chapter Six

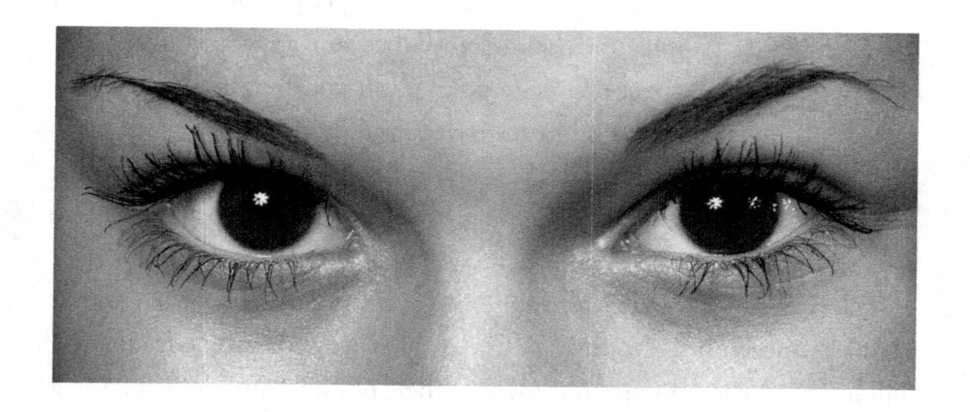

Details

"Peculiar I say, how so often the smallest, most seemingly insignificant details later unveil their faces as vital means for progression." [24]

Sherlock Holmes is a fictional character created by Sir Arthur Conan Doyle who first appeared in publication in 1887. By profession, the character of Holmes is that of a consultative detective, famous for his intellectual prowess, astute observation, and deductive reasoning. He makes use of his spare time in the study of botany, anatomy, geology, and chemistry, and is intimately familiar with every crime and horror perpetrated in the past century.

He has also made a study of specific items that people come in contact with such as the various types of tobacco and where each is sold, the type of soil present in different area of the city, types of medication including their proper or improper administration and possible side-effects.

---

[24] Criss Jami – Poet, philosopher and author.

As part of his deductive abilities, he recognizes behaviors and practices of people such as travelers, artisans, or people of various professions, foreigners, religious affiliations, etc...

The combination of knowledge and mental capabilities, coupled with his devotion to the scientific method, and commitment to asking questions, allows the infamous detective to identify important clues, and draw reasonable conclusions almost instantly. In short, Holmes is a sleuth.

When investigating a crime scene where someone had written a few words on a wall, the common observer might simply notice what words were written, but Sherlock Holmes would also observe the location on the wall, the angle of the words, the style of the writing, and even the choice of words used. This would give him an idea as to the height of the writer, evidence as to whether the person was right or left handed, and from their choice of words, an indication as to the person's level of education and possible place of origin.

Our ability to consider details is equivalent to learning to be like Sherlock Holmes. Our fictitious character is able to accomplish his amazing intellectual feats because he prepared himself through study and training to recognize various objects unique properties. Without this amazing collection of knowledge which he is able to draw upon when examining the details of a crime scene, Mr. Holmes would be no more capable as a sleuth than the average person.

Therein lays the secret. Mr. Holmes possesses both skills and knowledge. His skills at observation and deduction would have been ineffective without his extensive knowledge of various subjects upon which he applies his observation and deductive talent.

Attention to details is the next behavior in executing both more efficiently and effectively.

The level of detail associated with areas of interest that people study becomes the data the mind subsequently draws upon for deductive reasoning. The challenge is in determining the appropriate level of detail needed to successfully apply that knowledge. Excessive study in some areas can result in a waste of time gathering information that will have little practical value and be forgotten over time.

Consider, do you desire to be an expert in some field, or is your interest limited to that of a hobby. Either way, it is those little details that make things interesting.

The phrase, garbage in / garbage out, has literal meaning. The knowledge you acquire is the same knowledge you base your own behavior and any analysis of information that you might come upon. If what you take in is trivial junk, then all you will be able to apply in your efforts to be successful is that same useless junk.

Many people have tremendous analytic talent, but never gather sufficient data to fully analyze a situation and take the appropriate action. Many a politician has been elected by seemingly smart people who vote for an individual based on race, gender, or political affiliation without understanding the candidate's personal philosophy on key issues.

Other people gather and gather data, but fail to develop the analytical skills to apply that information effectively. Both detailed data and analysis are critical to understanding.

Researchers have discovered that lack of detail is why the best devised business strategies fail 67% of the time. A good executive knows that it isn't enough to set business objectives. There needs to be a detailed plan for achieving those objectives. As the saying goes, the devil is in the details.

Often leaders see a project, and focus only on the potential threats, and in doing so fail to recognize the host of great opportunities that are open to them. It is in the details where opportunities are discovered.

Attention to details also involves the quality of a product or service. Consider how a high quality restaurant sets its tables with linen napkins, place settings, and decorations verses what is seen at the common fast food establishments where hastily cleared tables are often still covered with crumbs of food, sticky substances, and dripping condiments.

Details communicate the level of craftsmanship associated with a piece of work or define the quality of a performance. They communicate how well things fit together.

In art a detail might involve the shade or color of an object. Detail brings out the unique and positive characteristics of a product. It is details that make personal appearance unique, thereby allowing us to distinguish between identical twins. It is the details that distinguish an original from a copycat, poor quality from high quality, mediocre from great.

By developing the behavior to exercise attention to details and craft a complete solution we differentiate the quality of our actions and work from the efforts of others. In short, our execution is better.

* * * * * * *

DEVELOP THE SLEUTH IN YOU

During the day, we all encounter moments where our normal activities get delayed or have gaps providing opportunities to do other things. Developing the ability to utilize important information requires the discipline to use those small moments of time that tend to slip by every day to increase your knowledge and understanding in areas you desire to excel.

Short periods of time quickly add up. By utilizing these moments, you can create an impressive collection of information that the mind can call upon to help improve the effectiveness of every performance.

While Sherlock Holmes is a fictional character, this keen ability to make observations and draw conclusions is a very real talent anyone can learn to develop.

Holmes companion and partner in solving mysteries is Dr. Watson whom Holmes utilizes frequently as a sounding board to clarify his analysis and penetrating thoughts. Watson serves to challenge Holmes thinking, and suggest alternatives. Having someone to share and bounce ideas off is an important element in working through the details of any task.

One of the biggest mistakes people make is in not finding someone to review a strategy or plan, or bounce ideas off of so as to verify the approach is sound before moving forward.

By opening ourselves to others feedback it is possible to discover holes in plans, gaps in understanding, and limitations that have been overlooked, and take action to correct the short sightedness before committing resources to executing a poorly conceived project.

The ability to communicate details is a critical factor in how well other people perceive a situation, interpret observations and draw conclusions before making their response. Detail is therefore not only needed in how we perceive the world, but in how others perceive these things.

Learning to pay attention to details is a simple matter of taking time to see beyond the obvious, and look below the surface. It begins by asking probing questions. For example;

What made a presentation interesting instead of boring?

What makes a stories plot compelling?

What detail sets two people apart from one another who otherwise exhibit very similar characteristics or attributes?

Why do some people command our attention when they enter the room, and others do not?

How can a task be done in a more effective manner?

The answer to these questions is found by examining the details to discover what is influencing different outcomes.

Consideration for detail forces us to look closer, to alter perceptions, explore new perspectives and consider alternative paradigms that make the difference in the ability to execute more effectively.

****

LOOK BEYOND THE OBVIOUS

There is a story about a man who stops to buy eggs from a farmer. As he was paying, he notices a large predator bird rousting in the chicken coop along with the chickens. Upon closer examination, the man recognizes it is a bald eagle and asks the farmer, "Why is that eagle in the chicken coop?"

The farmer explains that the bird was hatched from an egg he found, and placed in the coop. The bird had since grown up as a chicken. The man continues to observe the bird, and has to admit that the bird exhibits many of the characteristic behaviors of a chicken.

He eventually walks over to the cage and examines the bird which appears to be in good health. A thought then crosses his mind. Curious, the man asks if he can have the bird. Since it fails to lay eggs, prefers to eat raw meat, and occasionally scares the other animals due to its size, the farmer agrees.

The man carries the bird up onto a local hilltop where he takes it in both hands and tosses it into the air hoping to see it fly. Instead the bird slips to the ground, and pecks at the remains of a dead animal, still acting like a chicken.

The man next carries the bird higher up the mountain to a point overlooking the valley and farmer's home. He again tosses the bird up into the air, with the same result except that the bird glides partway down the mountain side.

The man decides to make a final attempt and takes the bird far up the mountain to the very top where he stands overlooking a steep craggy precipice. At this location the wind is blowing hard, and the air is filled with strong gusts and dangerous currents. There is a different smell to the air as the wind stirs and blends the various scents of the mountains foliage and wildlife. Far below, the farmer's home is just a speck among the many scattered buildings.

The man again lifts the bird, and for a few minutes holds it up where it can feel the strong cold air ruffle its feathers. It looks out to see in the distance the subtle movement of other forms of life undiscernibly to the man.

This time, before the man is able to toss it upward, the eagle spreads its wings. It feels the force of the wind flow over its feathers, and deep inside senses a grander purpose. With a single but sudden motion, the Eagle moves it wings taking it up and out over the precipice where it then begins to glide, then flies away into the distance.

The man returns to his vehicle with a feeling of joy in the experience of having served and freed the once caged bird.

So, what is this story about? Is it about an Eagle discovering itself? Most people think so, but they are wrong.

The key to understanding the story is in the details.

This is a story about a man buying eggs who recognized the true potential of a cooped up eagle. Unlike the farmer, the man sees more than a large bird in a cage.

He recognizes a bird with potential, and seizing an opportunity sacrifices his time, and after multiple attempts helps the bird discover what it truly is.

Had the man not observed a strange bird in the coop, or recognized its potential as an eagle, or not appealed to the farmer to let him have it, the eagle would in all likelihood have remained in the coop. With his purchase of eggs, the man could have simply driven off.

In that altered scenario, everyone would have concluded the story was obviously about a man buying eggs. The eagle elements are distractions that redirect our thoughts away from the man's actions.

It is a simple thing to look beyond the seemingly obvious to discover the truth of a matter, but most people are not willing to invest the appropriate amount of time. Human tendency is to see only the obvious, and fail to take action after first examining the details.

* * * * * * *

PENETRATE THE SMOKE

In military battles, combatants will drop special bombs or ignite flares that release large quantities of smoke as a tactic to shield their actions and confuse the enemy. With the smoke as a thin shield, soldiers can advance across an open area where they are exposed toward an objective with a moderate degree of assurance the enemy cannot target them.

Of course this screen of smoke also shields the enemy who could be hiding at the opposite edge of the field patiently behind the thick billowing cloud for a target to appear.

Depending on your perspective, the smoke screen can be either a blessing or a curse. When facing a smoke screen, those individuals with accurate detailed information have an advantage

When preparing to execute a task, the time to gather details begins well before you need them, not at the moment of execution when important decisions are required. By the time execution begins, smoke in the form of superfluous, emotional, or irrelevant information can obscure critical details. Advance gathering allows time to sort through the details, identify relevant elements, review and if necessary plan for or make adjustments. This way, at that decisive moment during execution, the plan can effectively go forward.

That said we all know that information is subject to change at the last moment. Critical details rarely change in a major way, so a last minute update is unlikely to generate a significant alteration of a plan. Still, it is essential that last minute updates be considered before making that final commitment to proceed.

Failure to recognize and address small details early can have major consequences later on. For example, before an airplane takes to the air, a short pre-flight check of the aircraft might reveal a loose component that if it were to fail during the flight would result in the aircraft crashing. Fixing the loose part before take-off would be a lifesaving event.

* * * * * * *

LEARN FROM MIRRORS

Of course not every piece of information involves researching details in other things. There is the need to also examine details about you.

When you look into a mirror, you perceive a reverse image of yourself. A mirror offers the chance to see yourself in a manner very similar to how others see you.

What do you see? Do you radiate success? Your attitude has a telepathic ability to communicate to others your abilities and desires. They can detect your enthusiasm, assess your willingness, evaluate your eagerness, but will challenge any hesitancy. These are important details.

Ask yourself questions like these;

Will people like what they see in me? This is not just physical appearance, but your character and personality.

How are they going to respond to your appearance? Will they find you attractive or plain looking?

How will your attitude be perceived? Are you happy, and pleasant? Do you seem frustrated or angry?

People respond to smiles and greetings positively, but avoid people who convey negativity or who seem glum.

Will they find you attractive? Attractive people find more opportunities because others enjoy associating with them, and assisting them in being successful.

Do you look professional, or casual? People who have a professional appearance are held in higher regard and their advice taken seriously.

* * * * * * *

Chapter Seven

Precision

Water freezes at 32 degrees Fahrenheit but remains a liquid at 33 degrees. A single degree makes all the difference.

Each year hundreds of thousands of young men around the world join and participate in a program that began in Great Britain known as the Boy Scouts. Since its origins, the program has grown and become available to young men around the globe. While some young men will be fortunate enough to save enough money to travel and attend the World Jamboree of Scouting, most will be limited to participating in activities in their home nations or community.

In the Boy Scouts of America, a common outdoor activity held in local councils is the semi-annual District Camporee.

Camporees allow all Boy Scout units within a geographical area to come together for a weekend to compete as organized patrols in performing traditional frontier skills such as rope making, first-aid, pioneering, fire building, knife and axe, and outdoor cooking. Some years the competition involves the challenge of completing in an orienteering course.

The orienteering activity involves following a series of compass bearings and pacing off distances to arrive as close as possible to a specific predetermined destination. This is not as easy as it might sound.

Teams begin at an assigned starting point. Each starting point has a unique destination. Each team will be required to take three or more sets of compass bearing and distance measurements to locate the final destination point. When obstacles block the path, it can require finding a way around the obstacle while still maintaining an accurate course.

Being off a single degree, or pacing a distance using a stride that is wrong by just a few inches can result in a significant variance from the final destination point.

In execution, like orienteering, precision is essential to an efficient, effective outcome. The directive to aim small, miss small, teaches a fundamental concept of precision.

Precision is the next behavior to improve in order to execute effectively.

The word precision means to be exact or accurate.

All of us have experienced the frustration of trying to assemble something that just doesn't quite fit together. It might have been an article of clothing where the buttons don't align with the holes, or a shelf where the supports are not level making the shelf tip slight toward one end or downward so items slide off.

The extent of error doesn't have to be much to miss the mark. When trying to piece things together, just a tiny measure of inaccuracy is sufficient to keep things from aligning properly. Every year millions of dollars are lost because a lack of precision stopped work, killing productivity.

The need for precision can easily be seen in sporting events. In the world of car racing, a small lapse in precision driving while vehicles accelerate around the race track can result in a crash with deadly consequences. In soccer, basketball, baseball, and football precision is a determining factor in the outcome, whether it be in defending a position, throwing the ball, or making a shot at the goal.

Precision is also critical in delivering a product or service while the window of opportunity is open. It doesn't do any good to have the window open, and miss the opportunity due to missing a critically timed delivery. When it comes to relationships, precision is a critical aspect. Too often the perceptions we might have of other people are imprecise resulting in misconceptions. Precision requires developing an attitude of ensuring information is factual and accurate before drawing conclusions.

A critical behavior for efficient execution is to perform each task precisely on the first attempt, thus eliminating the need to repeat the work or make late and costly corrections.

* * * * * * *

A STUDY IN PRECISION

What does precision require, and how does it impact the outcome?

You may have watched a television program where hidden cameras capture the behavior of people placed in unusual circumstances.

In one episode of a hidden camera show, a young sales woman is describing the various characteristics of a television set to a prospective buyer. The set is turned on and displays the sales floor area directly behind the television.

The gag being played on the perspective buyers is this. Each time the young sales woman steps behind the television, the image displays that portion of her body blocked by the television screen, as though she is wearing only underwear. It is as if the television magically filtered off layers of her clothing as she moves behind the TV. Of course, when she steps back to the side or in front of the television, the now unblocked portion of her body is still fully clothed. The televisions image continues in this manner displaying the scantily clothed parts of her body whenever the woman moves about behind the TV display.

To pull off the illusion, the woman's sales presentation was previously recorded for playback with her wearing only underwear. Her movements during the recorded video and her live clothed performance have to be identical, precise and perfectly in sync to create the illusion that her clothes are somehow being electronically filtered off her body whenever she moves behind the television. In this example, precision was essential to achieve the illusion.

In the example, several elements required precision.

First the women's movements had to be precisely identical for both the recorded and live presentation. The placement of her feet, and other body parts relative to the camera had to be exactly the same to create the illusion.

Second, the timing of her movements had to be precisely in sync between the recording and live presentation.

Third, the act had to be believable, not simulated or faked. A live performance made the illusion more believable.

The outcome of the gag was impressive as multiple customers were successfully drawn into observing the act and fooled by the illusion.

* * * * * * *

MEASURE TWICE, CUT ONCE

Precision is not only about the accuracy of physical equipment. A lot of the time information is communicated that isn't backed up by facts. Without accurate facts, the information being passed along will present a distorted picture.

People who do metalwork and woodworking understand the need for precision. There is no room for error in their craft.

Unlike scissors which severe cloth with a sharp edge, metal and woodworking tools work by chipping off very small pieces of the material that will settle on the floor as shavings or dust. Because a small amount of the material is lost, it is critical to make each cut at the precise spot. If a piece of material is cut wrong, the piece may be irreparably damaged. To prevent this, the craftsman learns to measure twice, and cut once.

Measuring twice is about validating information or checking that previous measurements were correctly performed before making a critical action.

Medical practitioners will recommend seeking a second opinion. Insurance carriers will often encourage multiple quotes before making repairs. Smart leaders align themselves with councilors who can provide support, or offer a second perspective prior to major critical decisions. Investigative journalist researching a story will seek a second source who can confirm the facts of a story before reporting

Measuring twice applies to every type of execution.

Successful execution involves gathering information and making intelligent decisions. Typically, the less information known the greater the level of precision required to account for the potential unknown detractors.

Of course the most accurate measurement is of little value if the tools being utilized lack the accuracy to perform the job. What good is a saw that doesn't cut straight, a square that doesn't form a perfect right angle, or a ruler that is not accurate?

A common mistake is proceeding when the information is incomplete or biased. If time permits, double check, or seek confirmation of the accuracy of information before finalizing plans. Try to explore options before settling on a solution.

Often our own perspective can be very biased. We make judgments based on our set of standards or values, our paradigm. We all carry emotional baggage, harbor negative memories, sometimes hold to different values, or suffer physical problems that cloud our perception. Because of this, avoid measuring someone or something by yourself assuming you have a complete and correct understanding. Get a second opinion. Eliminate bias by soliciting the viewpoint of other people, whose perspective *is different* than your own, and who can offer insights you may not be aware of.

When evaluating other people. It is easy to make a mistake and reach conclusions that like a piece of wood once cut, are impossible to repair.

Many employers, committees, board of directors, and work groups hire or select workers like themselves. The result is a lack of diversity in creative thinking. The ability to innovate is diminished. The target of their product or services ends up limited.

Years ago, a large church with global membership was developing a new hymn book for use in local congregational church services. The music selection committee was initially comprised exclusively of highly acclaimed music professionals nationally recognized for their talents. After a few meetings, the group wisely invited two individuals with little, if any, real musical experience to join them. These individuals initially felt intimidated by the high caliber of talented individuals who were part of the music selection team, and questioned the group's invitation to participate realizing their limitations at music. The response was that because these individual's had such limitations, they could best provide the perspective of the typical small meeting house congregations who in most meetings would be the person's attempting to sing the hymns. These people would require music appropriate for their musical skill level.

The point here is that a second opinion opens the means to achieving a better outcome.

* * * * * *

Chapter Eight

Attitude

Nothing can stop the man with the right mental attitude from achieving his goal; nothing on earth can help the man with the wrong mental attitude.[25]

Throughout the world, symbols or tokens of triumph have long been awarded to individuals and teams for the purpose of recognizing a superior accomplishment. It may be a plaque, laurel wreath, a blue ribbon, the gold cup, a medal, or some other badge of recognition. Years after the award is presented, the item will frequently or ultimately end up gathering dust in some display case or storage close, if not thrown out in the trash. The triumphant victory of the event it represents is

[25] Thomas Jefferson

typically long forgotten from the memories of both participants and spectators. The trophy is at best only a reminder that sometime in the past, a victory was achieved.

The problem with trophies is they can prevent us from being better at things we do. Wins are a temporary accomplishment achieved in that moment. It is easy to stop striving to improve once the trophy is awarded. The term we often hear describing those who live their life based on past accomplishments is known as resting on their laurels, a reference to the laurel wreath awarded to ancient athletic victors.

The good thing about trophies is they serve as a reminder that we have in the past demonstrated the ability to achieve success. When times get difficult and challenges seem insurmountable, being able to look back at an accomplishment and be reminded of what success feels like can be an emotional boost, and help change our attitude. One of the fundamental challenges we all face is recognizing the small daily successes that take place in our lives.

Trophies may be nice to receive, but they aren't needed as a reminder of how effective a person can perform and don't provide a measure of the level of proficiency in a skill.

A person's attitude is the true measure and indicator. Attitude is the final behavior associated with the simple things that influence our ability to execute effectively.

When it comes to executing, attitude is fundamental in determining how the work itself is achieved. Unlike a trophy, attitude can't gather dust, or be locked in a closet.

* * * * * * *

SPORTMANSHIP NOT DOMINANCE

Many companies in the business world describe themselves as the leader or dominate provider in their market. We often hear expressions in other various endeavors of crushing the competition. The question to consider has to do with whether dominance is essential to effective executing?

Years ago I participated in our church sponsored softball program. Local church units would assemble teams and compete each season with other teams in their local area. The top two teams would then be invited to a regional tournament from which the top two teams would advance to the area tournament. Finally the best teams in each area tournament would compete in a week long all-church softball tournament. Many of the best fast and slow pitch softball players in the country would show up with their team to participate in this prestigious event.

While in most sports the coveted first place trophy goes to the team or individual who wins the championship game, in the all-church tournament, the most coveted award was not for First Place or awarded to the team that won the championship game.

Instead, the highest award presented at the end of the tournament went to the team that exhibited the greatest level of sportsmanship during the competition. The coveted sportsmanship trophy recognized the team and individuals whose actions best championed the ideals of the sport itself.

Being a champion of the sport means being someone who emulates the best the sport has to offer. Sportsmen promote the game, encourage people to participate, and strive at all times to play by the rules in order to set and maintain the highest levels of integrity.

Sportsmanship requires maintaining an attitude of fellowship with one's competitors. You see your competitor as someone who forces you to do your very best. It doesn't mean you won't feel the pain of coming up short when losing. But you find yourself excited to have been a participant, and grateful for the experience. A powerful competitor helps take you to the next level by challenging you to work harder, smarter, and execute to your potential.

In her work entitled, No Excuses, The Fit Mind-Fit Body Strategy Book, Lori Myers makes the following points.[26]

"True sportsmanship is;

1) Knowing that you need your opponent because without him or her, there is no game.
2) Acknowledging that your opponent holds the same deep-rooted aspirations and expectations as you.
3) Knowing that, win or lose, you can walk off the playing field with satisfaction in your accomplishments.
4) Always taking the high road.
5) And always, always, always being a good sport."

These points speak to attitude. Winning is important. But executing with class and dignity always results in a winning lasting relationship.

****

KEEP SCORE

In the introduction, the attitude of doing verses trying was mentioned as a critical element of successful execution. Doing is not the same thing as winning, and doing is not just about completing the task. Doing is also about putting forth your best effort regardless of the outcome.

We realize that we will not always come out on top. There will be times when the competition is better, or unforeseen circumstances will create obstacles beyond one's current capability to overcome. In every field of competition, only one team or individual can win first place, but attitude is a thing that allows everyone to come out winning regardless of the final score.

---

[26] Lori Meyers is an entrepreneur and award winning writer who teaches that attitude is everything.

There is a saying that it doesn't matter whether you win or lose, but how you play the game.

Some people question this philosophy by asking, if it doesn't matter, then why bother keeping score?

The reason we keep score it to obtain a point of reference for each performance upon which to improve. As a project manager, a frequent area of discussion in my profession centers on continuous improvement. A point that is always stressed is that to measure improvement, a base or starting point is needed for comparison. Metrics are collected to see whether improvement is taking place. Keeping score is a simple metric of measure.

Paul Arden once said, "Ultimately, it's not how good you are. It's how good you want to be". [27]

Keeping score can occur in many ways. For example; someone wanting to lose weight might track their weekly level of physical activity, or count the calories they consume each meal. Sports teams gather and track hundreds of metrics on player's performance. Industries such as airlines and shipping companies track on-time arrival or deliveries in order to access the quality of their operational procedures.

Keeping score means collecting information and analyzing how work is being done to be more productive and improve on that performance.

Keeping score demonstrates an attitude of commitment to improving. It is a simple thing that shows others your dedication to overcoming obstacles faster and more effectively.

* * * * * * *

BE POSITIVE NOT OPTIMISTIC

There is a difference between being optimistic and exhibiting a positive attitude. Many people confuse the two.

[27] Paul Arden – Best quotes for life.

Optimism comes from the Latin word *optimus*, meaning “best”. Optimists expect the best outcome whereas positive thinkers anticipate a successful outcome.

Optimistic thinking focuses on the idea that everything will work out for the best by persisting and never giving in.

Optimism stems from and often produces an attitude of plan old stubbornness. A common trait of the optimist is to continue to pursue a bad approach even after it is clear to others that the approach is failing.

Why is this?

The optimist is certain in their thinking that the current approach will ultimately succeed if simply given enough time for the planets to align, fate to step in, or a miracle to take place. This characteristic stubbornness keeps the optimist from listening to others or exploring alternate choices.

Optimists can often take things very personally, particularly when the current approach is *their* approach, *their* thoughts and ideas, and therefore *their* accomplishment. Many will avoid ideas offered by anyone who challenges or question their view, certain in the successful outcome they anticipate. Optimists are waiting for something magical to occur and prove them right, even when the walls are falling down around them.

When execution begins to fail, optimists can carry a false illusion to the next higher levels, sometimes by assuming direct control hoping to prevent outsider interference that they perceive will negatively influencing the outcome.

This can foster conflict, as well as complacency, lower energy levels, and ultimately weaken execution. The optimists convinced of the approach resorts to creating the perception that all is going well, until it is too late and storms finally sink the ship. As the sinking ship disappears below the surface, they will find it hard not to have someone to blame for the failed outcome.

By comparison, positive thinking acknowledges the fact that problems can and probably will occur, in a manner that supposes things may not work out as planned. The positive thinker is realistic. By accepting this, positive people will begin the process of exploring alternate solutions to obstacles instead of allowing the current approach to bog things down in the hope of that magical miracle outcome occurring.

A positive attitude realizes that no problem is too large, only that a big challenge must be broken down to the point where each smaller obstacle can be overcome or worked around. The positive thinker isn't expecting to solve every problem, only enough problems to achieve the objective.

Positive thinking doesn't imply that negative thinking isn't occurring. In fact negative thinking is seen in a positive light as revealing potential risks and barriers. There are good things that can result from being skeptical, sad, angry, fearful, or experiencing other types of negative emotions.

The key to a positive attitude goes back to maintaining balance, which we addressed in the earlier chapters.

* * * * * * *

Printed in the United States
By Bookmasters

Printed in the United States
By Bookmasters